Transnational Institute

De Wittenstraat 25
1052 AK Amsterdam
The Netherlands
www.carbontradewatch.org
www.tni.org

First published February, 2007

Author
Kevin Smith

Contributors

Timothy Byakola	Chris Lang	Trusha Reddy
Jamie Hartzell	Oscar Reyes	

Editors
Oscar Reyes

Cover
Ricardo Santos

Design

Kevin Smith	Ricardo Santos	Zlatan Peric

Printing
Imprenta Hija de J. Prats Bernadás
Printed on 100 per cent recycled paper

The contents of this report can be quoted or reproduced as long as the source is mentioned. TNI would appreciate receiving a copy of the text in which this document is used or cited. To receive information about TNI's publications and activities, we suggest that you subscribe to our bi-weekly bulletin by sending a request to: tni@tni.org or registering at www.tni.org

To receive a monthly bulletin about news, reports and information about the world of emissions trading, carbon offsets and environmental justice, send an email to kevin@carbontradewatch.org or register at www.tni.org/ctw

Thank You: Karen, Mandy, Heidi, Fiona, Tami, Jutta, Larry, Vanja, Virginia, Matthais, Kolya, Tom, Nacho, Adam, Graham, Brianna and the Institute for Race Relations

ISBN 9789071007187

Contents

INTRODUCTION

From the late Middle Ages, Western Europe became slowly but surely engulfed by the tide of mercantilism that superceded the feudal economy. This system, which to us is second nature, was revolutionary at the time. It was, in its own way, the first wave of economic globalisation to wash over Europe.[1] Mercantilism, simply put, is a system of economic relations in which goods purchased in one place are sold at a much higher price somewhere they are scarce. The Catholic Church, at the time suffering from a shortage of funds, decided to use the burgeoning market ethic to its own material advantage.

Catholic doctrine maintains that to avoid time in Purgatory after you die, you need to expiate your sins via some sort of punishment or task that is an external manifestation of your repentance. The idea was that the clergy were doing more of such actions than their meager sins demanded, so they effectively had a surplus of good deeds. Under the logic of the emerging market, these could be sold as indulgences to sinners who had money, but not necessarily the time or inclination to repent for themselves. Chaucer's *The Pardoner's Tale* immortalised the sale of such indulgences by pardoners, which was essentially how the church took a market-based approach to sinning as a means of income generation. The Brazilian theologian Dr. Odair Pedroso Mateus pointed out in 2001 that indulgences are "not about grace and gratefulness but about exchanging goods, about buying and selling, about capitalism".[2]

Many centuries later, there are new indulgences on the market in the form of carbon offsets. The modern-day Pardoners are companies like Climate Care, the Carbon Neutral Company, Offset My Life and many others. These self-styled 'eco-capitalists' are building up what they claim are 'good climate deeds' through projects which supposedly reduce or avoid greenhouse gas emissions. These wholesale emissions reductions can then be profitably sold back at retail prices to modern-day sinners who have money, but not necessarily the time or inclination to take responsibility for their emissions, and can afford to buy the surplus 'good deeds' from the offset companies.

Most offset schemes take the following approach. A simple calculator on a website shows the quantity of emissions produced by a certain product or activity. The customer can then choose from a variety of projects that promise to 'neutralise' an equivalent amount of emissions by energy-saving, or through carbon absorption in trees. The consumer pays according to the claimed project costs and the amount of emissions to be 'neutralised'. Most carbon offset companies cater to both individuals and corporations. Corporations can pay to 'neutralise' emissions generated by the production of consumer items or services, which can then be marketed on the basis of their climate-friendly credentials. This process has been dubbed 'carbon branding'. The carbon offset market is booming. In the first three quarters of 2006, about EUR 89 million were sold to companies and individuals all over the world, up 300 per cent from 2005. It is predicted that the voluntary offsets market will be worth EUR 450 million in three years time.[3]

Even offset industry insiders are concerned about the lack of regulation and scrutiny of the new market. Offsets expert Francis Sullivan, who was instrumental in HSBC's attempt to 'neutralise' its emissions, commented that, "there will be individuals and companies out there who think they're doing the right thing but they're not. I am sure that people are buying offsets in this unregulated market that are not credible. I am sure there are people buying nothing more than hot air."[4] A report by Standard Life Investments on 'Carbon Management & Carbon Neutrality in the FTSE All-Share' tellingly warned that such schemes "have the capacity to disguise the failure to achieve actual reductions in overall greenhouse gas emissions."[5]

The Carbon Neutral Myth highlights several ways in which this approach to climate change is fundamentally flawed. The first chapter examines how the existence of offset schemes presents the public with an opportunity to take a 'business as usual' attitude to the climate change threat. Instead of encouraging individuals and institutions to profoundly change consumption patterns as well as social, economic and political structures, we are being asked to believe that paying a little extra for certain goods and services is sufficient. For example, if one is willing to pay a bit more for 'offset petrol' one doesn't have to worry about how much is consumed, because the price automatically includes offsetting the emissions it produces.

One of the most high-profile offset companies to emerge to date is the Carbon Neutral Company, formerly known as Future Forests. Chapter two examines its history, revealing mounting criticism of its business practice and exposing how little of its income makes it to the offset projects themselves.

The initial success of offset schemes was partly due to the popular idea that tree planting is inherently environmentally friendly. The third chapter criticises the scientific basis of offsetting, showing that it is not possible to equate absorption of atmospheric CO_2 by trees with the fossil CO_2 emitted from burning fossil fuels. It also examines problems with the impermanence of carbon storage in plantations, and how hypothesising what emissions have been avoided by renewable energy projects and emissions reduction schemes amounts to little more than guesswork.

The fourth chapter frames offset projects in the Majority World as a new stage in the Global North's coercive development agenda. Three case studies - plantations in India and Uganda, and an energy efficiency project in South Africa -show how the idealised portrayal of these projects is not always matched by the reality of the situation, either in terms of their effectiveness in reducing emissions or, more importantly, of their harmful impacts upon local communities.

Chapter five critically examines the use of celebrity endorsement in political environmental campaigns, which partly accounts for the enormous popularity of offsets. It includes interviews with two celebrities who have been more proactive in taking responsibility for their emissions, as well as touching on issues of climate change in their work.

The final chapter addresses the issue of providing positive alternatives rather than just criticising offset schemes. It draws attention to a company that has chosen other means of putting its green credentials into practice and, looking at the example of the recent victory of women in the Ogoni tribe of Nigeria against the petrol multinational Shell, examines why the solutions to climate change need to be much more systemic, empowered and politically engaged than is permitted within the scope of carbon offsets.

The sale of offset indulgences is a dead-end detour off the path of action required in the face of climate change. There is an urgent need to return to political organising for a wider, societal transition to a low carbon economy, while simultaneously taking direct responsibility for reducing our personal emissions. Offset schemes are shifting the focus of action about climate change onto lifestyles, detracting from the local participation and movement building that is critical to the realization of genuine social change. It is hoped that the rising awareness of the shortcomings of offset credits will contribute to a reformation of the climate change debate.

1 | CORRUPTING THE CLIMATE CHANGE DEBATE

"Every time we re-fuel, we're helping to care for natural assets"

At a very fundamental level, our success in dealing with climate change will depend on how quickly and profoundly we can change the way we live our lives, both collectively and individually. There is an urgent need to restructure society and our economies away from the 'business as usual' scenario of a fossil fuels-based, car-centered, throwaway economy to one that pragmatically reduces our emissions levels.

As an added imperative, there is considerable evidence that we are rapidly reaching our peak oil production. Global oil production has increased annually since oil was first extracted, and demand will almost certainly continue to rise while net production starts to decrease. Basic economic theory on supply and demand tells us that this widening gap, combined with the way in which cheap, abundant oil underpins so much of our industrial economy means that the consequences of reaching this oil production peak could be enormous.[1] With consumption levels in the global North far more intensive than those in the South, the most immediate and rational way to limit this chaos would be to take drastic steps to reduce the heavy fossil-fuel dependency of Northern countries.

Technology plays a crucial role in the necessary transition to a low-carbon economy, in terms of making our energy use more efficient, and in developing greater infrastructure for small-scale renewable energy. However, even a massive deployment of all of the available renewable energy technologies could still only generate a fraction of our current energy demand.[2] To help bridge this gap, the ongoing development of the technology-based response to climate change will need to be met by a sea-change in cultural values, with the implementation of climate-friendly technologies taking place alongside dramatic cuts in energy consumption levels. This implies a wider cultural transformation, so that society accords high esteem to energy and climate conscious behaviour and discourages waste and extravagance. In this scenario, driving an urban SUV or taking short-haul flights for frivolous reasons would be seen as irresponsible and antisocial, just as we now see littering or drink-driving. Keeping up with the Joneses would mean installing the most efficient mini-wind turbine rather than having the biggest wide screen TV. This hegemonic shift towards the primacy of climate-friendly values in popular opinion would be necessary in order for governments to take the difficult decisions involved in seriously cutting emissions levels while still retaining credibility and support from their electorate.

'Business-as-usual' is not an option

A necessary starting point for bringing about this change in society is to acknowledge that the 'business as usual' scenario cannot continue. This is why the culture of offsets is corrosive to the climate change debate. It presents itself as a way that people can effectively deal with climate change while largely maintaining their levels of energy consumption. Instead of acknowledging the uncomfortable but necessary truth that we cannot responsibly persist with our current lifestyles, climate-conscious people are being encouraged to believe that with offset schemes they can continue as they were, as long as they pay money to absolve themselves of their responsibility to the climate.

Public figures and politicians are sending out a message that offsets present a valid alternative to taking a serious approach to climate change. In January 2007, Tony Blair received criticism in the media when he said in response to calls to cut down on his personal flights that, "I personally think these things are a bit impractical, actually to expect people to do that."[3] A few days later, realising that his green credentials had been tarnished, he hastily announced that he would be paying to 'offset' his family holidays.

"Offsetting is a dangerous delaying technique because it helps us avoid tackling the task [of dealing with climate change]," reported Kevin Anderson, a scientist with the Tyndall Centre for Climate Change Research. "It helps us sleep well at night when we shouldn't sleep well at night. If we had gone to the limit of what we can do in our own lives then I could see it would be a route to go down, but we've not even started to make changes to our behaviour. I'm sure the people attending the G8 summit didn't need a separate limo and Merc each to pick them up. But to then claim that the problem is dealt with by planting a couple of trees or whatever is worrying".[4]

Some of the offset companies who wish to present themselves as being more responsible take care to mention that offsetting is only a part of the service that they offer, and that it should be pursued only in conjunction with implementing energy efficiency measures and reducing energy consumption where possible. However this is often in the equivalent of the small print. In almost all cases the media promotes only the act of offsetting and not, except when responding to criticism, the less glamorous business of making lifestyle changes.

Moreover, to date, there have been no offset schemes that encourage individuals to engage in collective action or political organising to bring about wider structural change. The structure of such schemes means that the onus for climate action is placed entirely on individuals acting in isolation from others. This inhibits their political effectiveness. Offset schemes assign a financial value to people's impetus to take climate action, neatly absorbing it into the prevailing logic of the market. Once you can click and pay the assigned price for 'experts' to take cost-effective action on your behalf, there remains little need to question any of the underlying assumptions as to the nature of the social and economic structures that may have brought about climate change in the first place.

And for every offset company that mentions that offsets should only be part of the response to climate change, there is another that will make sweeping claims that you "can neutralise the greenhouse emissions from your home, office, car and air travel in 5 minutes and for the cost of a cappuccino a week,"[5] and that "modern living needn't cost the earth".[6] People who may wish to pay money to offset even the environmental costs of that cappuccino can visit www.offsetmylife.com where offsets for every aspect of modern life are in development, from drinking coffee to watching television.

Delaying the transition

Other offset schemes are utilised by industries whose profit margins depend on delaying the transition to the low-carbon economy for as long as possible. For petrol companies and airlines, offsets represent an opportunity to 'greenwash'[7] their activities. It is possible to use 'carbon branding' through offset schemes to present the types of human activity that directly exacerbate climate change as being effectively 'neutralised,' and with no impact on the climate. So British Airways, which opposes aviation taxes and would never advocate that people simply choose not to fly unnecessarily can, through Climate Care, present its climate-conscious passengers with the option of flying free from concern over the impact of their emissions. This shift to what is essentially an unregulated and disputed form of eco-taxation away from the company and onto the consumer has gained British Airways an enormous amount of favourable publicity.

"At a time when some airlines are burying their heads in the sand over global warming, British Airways is tackling the issue full on," proclaimed the director of Climate Care, while Elliot Morley MP, the UK Government minister for climate change and environment, urged all air travellers to consider offsetting their flights.[8]

In the time that British Airways has been in partnership with Climate Care, it has also been vigorously promoting the massive expansion of British airports, has launched its own budget airline to short-haul holiday destinations, and has increased its inter-city commuter flight services. British Airways reported a £620m pre-tax profit for the year ending March 2006, a 20 per cent increase on the previous year, despite the increase in fuel costs during the period, and its short haul service moved into profit for the first time in a decade.[9] This was a period of expansion and profitability as much for Climate Care as it was for British Airways. In July 2006, Climate Care's David Wellington wrote that "in the past 10 to 12 months we have seen a 10-fold increase in sales," and that 85 per cent of this growth was in "online sales for offsetting flight emissions".[10]

Several services aimed at car drivers have adopted a similar approach. Terrapass, a US-based offsets website, encourages its users to think that "me and my car are doing something good for the planet", instead of encouraging people to critically evaluate the climate change impact of their driving patterns.[11] In July 2006, Climate Care and Land Rover announced "the largest and most comprehensive CO_2 offset programme ever undertaken by an automotive manufacturer in the UK,"[12] offsetting both the emissions generated by the production of vehicles, and also providing a mechanism for drivers of the vehicles to offset their fuel use. This scheme provides a critical piece of greenwash for the 'offroad' four-wheel drive, or Sports Utility Vehicles (SUVs), which have become almost emblematic of the head-in-the-sand approach to climate change. A 2004 academic report commissioned by Greenpeace, which focuses largely on Land Rovers, shows that vehicles "designed for offroad terrain consume 300 per cent more fuel, emit 300 per cent more pollution and, in an accident, are three times more likely to kill a pedestrian than an ordinary passenger car". The report also concludes that "while the urban SUV driver may be irresponsible, the real villains are the car manufacturers who market even bigger, heavier and more polluting cars".[13]

Land Rover's parent company, Ford, is also the target of a campaign by the US-based Rainforest Action Network due to its appalling track record on energy consumption and climate change. A 2004 report by the Union of Concerned

Scientists showed that Ford has the worst greenhouse gas pollution performance of all the 'Big Six' auto-industry companies in the US. According to the US Environmental Protection Agency, the average fuel efficiency of Ford's fleet today is 19.1 miles per gallon, placing it last among the major automakers.[14] For a company receiving so much criticism from environmental groups, the positive publicity gained by a partnership with a company like Climate Care is of enormous value.

State of the art greenwash

Offset schemes as a means to assuage consumers' concerns about their fossil-fuel use have reached their logical conclusion with the case of BP's Global Choice scheme in Australia. Motorists purchasing BP Ultimate, a sulphur-free petrol, are told that the price includes a contribution to Global Choice through which "BP will automatically offset 100 per cent of your emissions at no extra charge to you".[15] The message here is unqualified: if you purchase BP Ultimate, you no longer have to worry about the impact of your petrol's emissions because BP is taking care of it for you. This message is reflected in the advertising of companies involved with the Global Choice programme: "Every time we re-fuel, we're helping to care for Australia's natural assets... it's nice to know that your Australian adventure is giving something back to nature!" as the publicity for Backpacker Campervan Rentals puts it.[16]

BP's use of marketing and re-branding to portray itself as having excellent green credentials has been extensively documented and discredited. In 2000, a year after BP bought out Solarex, the world's largest manufacturer of solar panels, for $45 million, it spent more than four times as much on re-branding itself with the green-sounding slogan "Beyond Petroleum", and a series of adverts emphasising its alternative energy credentials.[17] The development of its offset programme was an ideal opportunity for BP to engage in cutting edge greenwash. "I think that most people in the oil industry are actually very, very green and want to do the right thing, it's just how can you do that?" said Mike McGuinness, BP's vice president for fuels management in Australia. "Until I got involved with clean fuels I couldn't see how I could make a difference".[18]

The afterlife of the BP Ultimate scheme provides a clear illustration that greenwashing, rather than a genuine attempt to address climate change, remained its underlying motivation. While the programme initially applied to all purchasers of BP Ultimate, it was later scaled down and applied exclusively to commercial users of the company's fuel credit cards. Although Kerryn Schrank,

BP's business adviser for future fuels, claimed that "we fundamentally believe that we need to tackle climate change," he went on to admit that the operation was scaled back because "very few people had heard of the programme and, even if they had, they didn't understand it... We were spending a lot of money purchasing offsets for a customer base who had no idea we were doing it for them."[19] The impetus to tackle climate change, even through a very dubious methodology like offsetting, was not as fundamental as presenting the appearance of doing so to BP's customers.

The use of offsets by companies like BP can conveniently draw attention from a disastrous track-record of environmental and human rights abuses. In July 2006, BP reported record second-quarter profits of $6.1bn (£3.3bn), its profits surging ahead despite a disastrous run of events in the preceding period which, in March 2005, included a refinery explosion that killed 15 workers and injured 170 in Texas, and an $81m settlement following charges it had released toxic gases from a refinery in California.[20] In March 2006 BP was responsible for a 270,000-gallon oil spill in Proudhoe Bay, America's biggest oilfield on Alaska's North Slope. In August, BP suspended production at 57 wells at Prudhoe Bay after whistleblowers alleged they were leaking. In the same month, the company was served a subpoena by the attorney general of Alaska ordering it not to destroy documentation connected to the corrosion of the leaking pipelines after allegations were made that BP had avoided having to replace parts of ageing pipelines by manipulating inspection data.[21]

From flights, to four-wheel drives, to petrol itself, carbon offsets provide a false legitimacy to some of the most inherently unsustainable products and services on the market. What's more, the costs of this purchasable legitimacy are often largely shunted onto the consumer, who effectively ends up paying for the greenwash. These companies also benefit because offset schemes place more of the focus on the consumers' responsibility for climate change - at the expense of examining the larger, systemic changes that we need to bring about in our industries and economies.

2 | THE RISE AND FALL OF FUTURE FORESTS

The first carbon offset project was organised in the US in 1989, when Applied Energy Services had its plans to build a 183 megawatt coal-fired power station approved partly due to its pioneering offset, which involved planting 50 million trees in the impoverished Western Highlands of Guatemala. This initial project was beset by many of the problems that have plagued offset schemes ever since. The non-native trees that were planted initially were inappropriate for the local ecosystem and caused land degradation. The local people had their habitual subsistence activities, such as gathering fuel wood, criminalised. Ten years on from the start of the project, evaluators concluded that the offset target was far from being reached.[1]

Some years later, the Future Forests company was born around a campfire backstage at the 1996 Glastonbury Music Festival.[2] Company founder and former music promoter Dan Morrell and the late Joe Strummer of legendary punk band The Clash conceived of the idea of planting trees to offset the emissions of climate-damaging gases. Despite a rash of negative publicity in recent years, Future Forests (now, re-branded as the Carbon Neutral Company) set precedents as the first high-profile offset company to emerge, garnering a great deal of press through the high-profile patronage of pop stars and famous actors, brought in through Morrell's and Strummer's connections to the entertainment industry. The first high profile clients were the Rolling Stones, who publicised the 2,800 trees that would offset emissions from their 2003 UK tour.[3] This was based on the calculation that it would take one tree to offset the emissions of 57 fans. It should be noted that this provided much-needed positive press coverage for the band after it was revealed that its support act for the German leg of the same tour had fascist links.[4]

For a while it seemed that celebrities were falling over themselves to get in on the act. In 2004, Brad Pitt paid Future Forests $10,000 to maintain a forest in his name in the kingdom of Bhutan to offset his carbon-intensive Hollywood life-style, while the actor Jake Gyllenhaal gave a similar sum for the carbon rights to a tree plantation in Mozambique. The Future Forests concept was also opened up to the not so rich and famous. Music fans can "follow the excellent environmental example set by Coldplay" by paying to dedicate a mango tree in a plantation in Karnataka, India,[5] while similar celebrity-branded forests were endorsed by the likes of Simply Red, Dido and Iron Maiden.[6] Corporate clients of Future Forests, who paid to share the supposedly positive, eco-conscious limelight generated by the celebrities, included Sainsbury's, BP, Fiat, Mazda, Audi, Barclays and Warner Brothers.

The difference between green action and greenwash

During the same period, a number of critical voices began to emerge, questioning both the validity of the science involved in offsetting emissions, in particular by planting trees, and the amount of money from offset purchases that actually made it to the projects themselves. In May 2004, a coalition of environmental and social justice groups (including Carbon Trade Watch) sent letters to several Future Forests clients asking them to reconsider their association with the company, arguing that the "difference between planting trees, which benefits the climate, and planting trees as part of a programme sanctioning further fossil fuel burning" is the "difference between green action and greenwash".[7]

At the same time formal complaints were made to the British Advertising Standards Authority over claims made by Future Forests in adverts in a Tower Records outlet and in Barclays Bank. The British Code of Advertising requires that any "significant division of scientific opinion" is reflected in any claims made by an advertisement, and the complaints alleged that the 'fierce' scientific controversy surrounding the use of tree plantations was not represented in the adverts.

The company was also criticised for misleading the general public into thinking that its payments fully funded the planting of extra trees. In fact, Future Forests was paying only a minor supplement towards the planting of already-planned trees. For instance, a 2001 contract between Future Forests and a forestry enterprise established on public land in North Yorkshire in the UK specified that while the company did not acquire ownership of "individual trees" it was entitled to "individual separable, enforceable... carbon sequestration rights in the land".[8]

In an article in the *Sunday Times* in 2005, the Chief Executive of a tree-planting charity called Trees For Cities criticised Future Forests: "Pop stars think they are paying to get trees planted. Really what they are doing is paying for a marketing company to go out and buy carbon rights on trees that other people are planting."[9]

Future Forests has generally relied on the publicity generated by celebrity endorsements to sell its products, rather than more traditional advertising methods. Mass media reports that a star was paying money to Future Forests in order to 'neutralise' an album or a tour or for their flights this year would effectively advertise Future Forests. People would see the name, visit the website and buy the offset products. The strategy was a clever one in that Future Forests could not be held legally responsible for any misrepresentation of its services in the media. This was key because it allowed Future Forests to be continuously misrepresented as planting new trees rather than buying the carbon rights to existing ones. Whether out of a desire to 'dumb down' or out of simple ignorance, journalists invariably reported that trees had been planted as a direct result of money the celebrities had paid.

Pauline Buchanan Black of the Tree Council, an umbrella group of 150 organisations, which often acts as a UK government adviser on forestry issues, said: "Members say they have been approached [by Future Forests] for the sale of carbon rights which is different to planting trees and sometimes those trees have been planted with resources from other sources. On their website they talk of planting trees and say they have helped to plant over 90 forests. Our members are very concerned that they are not planting trees."[10]

Future Forests has not made its contracts with forestry companies publicly available. However, in late 2005, using the UK's new Freedom of Information Act, Trees For Cities obtained a copy of the carbon sequestration agreement that had been made between the Highlands and Islands Enterprise (HIE) and Future Forests in 2002.[11] The Orbost forest, managed by the HIE, was one of the largest forestry sites used by Future Forests and featured heavily in their promotional literature. The agreement showed that Future Forests paid £34,275 for the carbon sequestration rights in 80 hectares of woodland - just £428 per hectare, which equates to around 43 pence per tree.[12] On the official Rolling Stones website, it states that "more than 2,000 world-wide fans have paid £8.50 each to plant trees at Orbost."[13] On the basis of these calculations, this would have amounted to £16,140 going to the profits and overheads of Future Forests, and just £860 to the forest.

From Future Forests to the Carbon Neutral Company

In September 2005, Future Forests re-branded itself as the Carbon Neutral Company. This was claimed to be a result of the company emphasising activities other than forestry offset projects. Climate change consultancy and offset projects based on renewable energy and energy efficiency had apparently become the focus. However, the change happened at a time when a lot of unfavourable publicity was associated with the name Future Forests. It is testament to the efficiency of their marketing that despite their being so much controversy and criticism, that the company still occupies a prominent place in the offsets industry. The company has gained further legitimacy by acting as the secretariat in the All Party Parliamentary Climate Change Group, which works "closely with businesses in order to develop policy options that will work to more fully integrate government and business in tackling climate change."[14]

In some ways, the criticism that forestry offset credits have received mirrors the move away from using forests and tree-plantations as 'carbon sinks' under the Kyoto Protocol. Although a large part of the treaty provided a framework for using 'carbon sinks' to gain carbon-credits so that signatory countries could keep emitting fossil carbon, concerns about scientific unreliability and the inability to guarantee the permanence of the trees have so far kept the use of these trees and forests as carbon sinks out of the offset market related to the Kyoto Protocol. However, the EU is keen to overturn the ban that has so far kept sinks credits out of the European Emissions Trading Scheme, and there are moves afoot to change the rules in order to allow already existing forests to generate official Kyoto credits. Pressure is also being applied in the official negotiations for trees that have been genetically modified to absorb more CO_2 to receive more credits under the Kyoto Protocol.

As a result of the negative publicity that trees as carbon offsets generally, and Future Forests specifically, have received in the press, many offset companies have now distanced themselves from tree planting projects, preferring to focus on projects involving renewable energy and energy efficiency. The various problems of all these different types of offset projects are explored in greater detail in the next chapter.

The move away from plantation-based offsets is not necessarily a permanent trend. The voluntary offset market is still relatively new, and some industry insiders feel that they are currently exploiting only the tip of the iceberg. Ingo Puhl, managing director at German offset provider 500ppm, said that "in terms of overall market potential, we [the voluntary offset industry] are tapping less than 1 per cent".[15]

If there was to be such enormous growth in the voluntary offset market, then it would need enormous expansion of both energy and forestry offset projects in order to satisfy demand. In addition, to date there has been limited criticism of energy offset projects in comparison to forestry projects. The Carbon Neutral Company's CEO Jonathon Shopley observes that, "pendulum is currently swinging away from forestry. People seem more comfortable with technology. Once people understand that there are complex issues related to technology offsets that we haven't really grappled with yet... I'm reasonably sanguine that forestry sequestration will be there."[16]

3 | THE PROBLEMS WITH TREES AND LIGHT BULBS

The idea of carbon offsets hinges on a simple equation, and its simplicity is part of its appeal. On one side of the equation you have CO_2 emissions, which are relatively straightforward to measure. The websites of offset companies usually offer a calculator device, which instantly converts details of your car journey or flight into a figure of how much you need to pay for. Unfortunately, it's just not that simple. It is impossible to accurately quantify the amount of CO_2 that has been supposedly 'neutralised'. With plantation-based projects, our knowledge of the carbon cycle is too limited to be able to assess just how much CO_2 is being absorbed by trees. With all offset projects, including the energy-efficiency and renewable energy-based ones that are being promoted as being more reliable than plantations, it is impossible to accurately assess just how much extra CO_2 there would have been in the atmosphere had the project not existed.

Complexities of the carbon cycle

Part of the success of the Carbon Neutral Company and many other offset schemes is that they exploit the popular notion that planting trees is, by definition, a 'good thing'. Trees are strongly symbolic of green politics, with many environmental groups like the US-based Sierra Club using trees in their logos. The UK Conservative party in 2006 adopted a tree as its new logo in an attempt to bolster its green image. To call somebody a 'tree-hugger' is to describe them as being ecologically-sensitive. The idea of planting trees in order to 'neutralise' emissions taps into a pre-existing cultural notion that something with obvious environmental benefits could be used to cancel out doing something environmentally damaging.

But it just doesn't add up.

CO_2 is absorbed by trees as part of the carbon cycle, an incredibly complicated set of chemical, physical, geological, and biological processes passing carbon through the earth's biosphere. The carbon cycle can be divided into two parts: active and inert. Trees are part of the active carbon cycle, a continual movement of carbon among plants, organisms, water and the atmosphere. In contrast, reserves of fossil fuels are inert: the carbon they contain is locked up and does not come into contact with the active part of the carbon cycle unless we burn them. Movement of carbon between the active cycle and the inert pool is one-way - once carbon is released from the inert pool by burning fossil fuels, it enters the active cycle. It will not return to the inert pool unless it undergoes the same sort of millennia-long geological process that transformed it into a fossil fuel in the first place.

This fact holds numerous implications for plantation offsets. Firstly, there is scientific uncertainty surrounding the complicated exchanges of the active part of the carbon cycle. There is a huge degree of variation in estimates of how much CO_2 trees are capable of absorbing and for how long they store how much of it, so it is impossible to tell with any degree of accuracy how many trees you would need to plant in order to accurately 'neutralise' your emissions.

One of the more recent examples of this scientific uncertainty was a study published in Nature in January 2006, which showed that trees and plants are responsible for emitting a lot more methane (another of the greenhouse gases responsible for climate change) into the atmosphere than had been previously thought, contributing something in the region of 10 to 30 per cent of the annual total of methane entering the earth's atmosphere. Dr. Richard Betts of the Hadley Centre, a climate monitoring organisation, commented that while the research would not greatly influence predictions of global average temperature, "it shows how complicated it is to exactly quantify reforesting or deforesting in comparison with current fossil fuel emissions".[1]

A study published in December 2006 by the Carnegie Institution of Washington in Stanford, California concluded that most forests do not have any overall impact on global temperature. "The idea that you can go out and plant a tree and help reverse global warming is an appealing, feel-good thing," said Ken Caldeira, a co-author of the study, "to plant forests to mitigate climate change outside of the tropics is a waste of time."[2]

At some point, when the tree is burnt, or its wood decays, the carbon will be released back into the atmosphere. Dr. Kevin Andersen from the Tyndall Centre for Climate Change Research raises a critical question: "Even if the trees do survive, if we have climate change and a 2° C or 3° C temperature rise, then how do we know those trees are not going to die early and break down into methane and actually make the situation worse?"[3]

In October 2006, the UK Advertising Standards Authority (ASA) underlined this scientific uncertainty when it ordered the Scottish and Southern Energy Group (SSE) to stop making claims about 'neutralising' its customers emissions in its leaflets. In the contentious leaflet, the SSE claimed that, "we plant trees to balance out the CO2 that your gas heating and household waste produces". SSE had contracted the World Land Trust to plant 150,000 trees over a three year period, and planting had already begun in Brazil and Ecuador. Although the SSE was able to provide the figures on how many emissions the average household produced, the lack of scientific knowledge about the carbon cycle meant that it was unable to provide sufficient proof that the number of trees that it planted would match or exceed the level of emissions.[4] It remains to be seen what impact this ruling will have on similar claims made by other offset schemes.

Anything could happen in 99 years

Some offset companies like The Carbon Neutral Company promise to "ensure that woodlands are created and well-managed over a minimum of 99 years".[5] The details as to how such long-term guarantees are to be enforced are not given. Critics argue that such guarantees are almost impossible to make, especially in light of the small amounts of money that are invested in the planting relative to the long-term costs of their maintenance. In 2003, the Chief Executive of the London-based Tree For Cities charity wrote a letter to The Daily Telegraph saying that Future Forests had offered them 50 pence (€ 0.75) to plant a tree and maintain it for 99 years. He added, "The real cost for this would be at least £5 per tree, meaning that Future Forests was offering us at best 10 per cent of the real cost. It would then sell-on the tree that we plant, paid for largely through charity donations that we have raised, for around £5 to £10 to the likes of Leonardo DiCaprio, Working Title, Avis and O2 to badge and claim as their 'tree'. This clearly is not additional. We rejected Future Forests' offer of 50p per tree because we have no intention of using our charitable donations to subsidise its business."[6]

These long-term legal contracts mean that land and water are not simply being commandeered in the name of offsets in the present. Such projects are also staking a claim on the future. In *Carbon Trading: A Critical Conversation on Climate Change, Privatisation and Power*, Larry Lohmann points out that offset projects "divert not only present but also future resources to licensing and prolonging fossil fuel use".[7]

The fact that the trees are supposed to absorb the carbon over a period of 99 years also raises a serious issue over timing. Many climate scientists have emphasised that the next decade is a critical period for emissions reductions, if we are to avoid crossing a threshold of global temperature increase that would create feedback loops amplifying the impact of climate change.[8] The atmospheric carbon released by cars and flights is already contributing to emissions, while offset projects that rely on far longer periods of carbon absorption will, hypothetically, be lowering emissions levels after this critical period for action has passed.

Even if the idea of planting trees as a means of offsetting emissions were to be taken seriously, rather than approached as a gimmicky piece of greenwash, there would be problems, since issues of land scarcity would have to be addressed. Where would all these plantations go? Putting aside all of the other problems of offsets and plantations for a moment, the figures don't add up. If we were to pretend that tree planting was a relevant way to reduce emissions, then it would require about 10,000 km2 of new plantations each year to absorb the UK's annual emissions, an area roughly the size of Devon and Cornwall, and these new forests would need to be maintained indefinitely.[9]

Such a scenario is clearly implausible, but it nevertheless raises important questions about where the land for all these plantations will come from and what means will be used to obtain it. In the UK, the Carbon Neutral Company has a number of offset projects on Forestry Commission land, which is the property of the state, effectively privatising what should be public carbon.

Baselines and speculations - the underlying uncertainty of all offsets

Following the torrent of negative publicity carbon offset plantations have received, some offset companies have been keen to either limit the proportion of tree planting projects in their portfolios (both the Carbon Neutral Company and Climate Care now say they aim to have no more than 20 per cent of their offsets derived from plantations[10]) or to focus exclusively on projects based on renewable energies or emissions reduction. These projects are still subject to the underlying problem of all offset projects, however, which is that it is simply not possible to accurately quantify emissions reductions when you are reliant on such speculative scenarios.

The credits that an offsets project generates are calculated by subtracting the emissions of the world that has the project in it from the emissions of an otherwise-identical possible world that doesn't. This last world represents the 'baseline'. The quantity of offsets credits that are generated and available to sell is equivalent to the emissions reductions beyond this baseline.

In order for the system to work, this baseline has to be accurately determined. Without an accurate baseline, sellers wouldn't know how much of their commodity they were actually selling, and buyers wouldn't know how much they were buying. The assessment by experts and verifiers of the hypothetical scenario without the project is, at best, informed guesswork. Many without-project scenarios are always possible. As Larry Lohmann points out in his treatise on carbon trading, "The choice of which one to be used in calculating carbon credits is a matter of political decision rather than economic or technical prediction."[11]

There are innumerable factors that could alter the baseline of the without-project scenario, such as socio-economic trends, future land use, demographic changes and international policymaking. As Jutta Kill from the FERN campaign network points out, "if the carbon market had been active in 1988 then East Germany would have been a prime target for energy saving projects. But how many predictions of baseline emissions would have included the fall of the Berlin wall the following year?"[12]

Much of the baseline speculation relates to the principle of 'additionality' - that is, the idea that the project would not have happened without the funding from the offset companies. In the next chapter, an offsets project by Climate Care to distribute low-energy light bulbs in South Africa is examined, in which residents of a township would have received the light bulbs regardless of the involvement of Climate Care. A report by the Royal Institute for International Affairs flatly acknowledges the "impossibility of measuring and defining savings that are additional to those that would have occurred in the absence of emissions credits."[13]

A more definite resolution to the question of whether or not a project would have happened anyway "seems as elusive as ever", according to Mark Trexler, a climate change business consultant. "There is no technically 'correct' answer," he concedes. "Never has so much been said about a topic by so many, without ever agreeing on a common vocabulary and the goals of the conversation."[14]

While scientists, using appropriate instruments and calibrations, are able to agree on how to directly measure real emissions, there is no consensus possible on how to accurately choose one genuine baseline out of the multitude of possibilities and calculate the hypothetical emissions reductions from it. The lack of verification about baselines also means that there are enormous incentives and opportunities for companies to employ creative accountancy to choose a baseline that would result in larger numbers of sellable credits to be generated on paper.

Future value accounting

The credibility of all offsets projects is further undermined by the fact that today's emissions are not the equivalent of emissions being 'neutralised' over a period of time. The reason why the offset companies can argue for carbon neutrality is they are using a carbon calculation method that is best termed 'future value accounting'. Carbon savings expected to be made in the future are counted as savings made in the present. This is the same technique used by Enron to inflate its profits with such disastrous consequences. Each time someone offsets their emissions, the amount of CO2 emitted is automatically in the atmosphere, whereas the period of 'neutralisation' takes place over a much-longer time period, sometimes 100 years. If that person keeps offsetting regularly, their rate of emissions increases rises at a much faster rate than the rate at which their activities are being 'neutralised' to the point at which, far from being climate neutral, quite the opposite is true. The carbon in the atmosphere increases at a far greater rate than it's supposed 'neutralisation'. A more graphic and detailed explanation of this 'future value accounting' is given in the appendix.

Carbon colonialism

In addition to voluntary offset companies' schemes, a parallel process at the international level under the Kyoto Protocol allows large companies to buy their way out of reducing their emission reductions targets by investing in 'climate-friendly' projects and schemes in countries in the Majority World that are supposed to neutralise the gases that are emitted in the Northern countries. Some of these projects are also tree plantations, or 'carbon sinks' as they are referred to in the Kyoto agreement. All of the arguments that we have examined are equally relevant to this sort of offsetting on a larger scale under Kyoto, but these proposed larger scale plantations bring the issue of land-rights and social justice even more sharply into focus.

Critics from groups such as FERN, the World Rainforest Movement, the Green Desert Movement and Rising Tide have portrayed the use of monoculture tree plantations in the Majority World to 'neutralise' the emissions of the Northern world as a form of 'carbon colonialism',[15] whereby resources of countries in the Majority World (in this case, the land used for plantations) are used in order to maintain the levels of material privilege (in this case, high levels of energy consumption) enjoyed by Northern countries. The report *The Carbon Shop* illustrates how such plantations are an extension of the colonial mindset that has already wreaked havoc in a number of countries in the search for fossil-fuels and other such plunder: "Ironically, the community evicted today by a company drilling oil to feed distant automobiles may find itself displaced again tomorrow - this time by tree plantations intended by the drivers of those automobiles to 'offset' the burning of that oil".[16]

There is a growing body of evidence detailing the damage done to communities and ecosystems through plantation projects in the Majority World. A study published in *Science* magazine in 2005 included 500 observations from plantations on five continents, and showed that tree planting had negative impacts on local biodiversity through absorbing large quantities of groundwater, and by depleting essential soil nutrients.[17] There has also been a great deal of research into the damage that plantations proposed as offsets can cause to local communities in countries such as Ecuador,[18] Brazil[19] and India.[20]

The various offset companies have cast their net wide in implementing projects in the Majority World. The Carbon Neutral Company currently has projects in Mexico, Mozambique, India, Uganda and Bhutan;[21] Carbon Clear funds tree planting projects in India and Tanzania;[22] while Climate Care is funding a forestry project in Uganda.[23] The next chapter takes a closer look at some specific case studies, showing how these projects have had negative impacts on local communities and have often been ineffective in dealing with climate change.

4 | THREE PROJECTS IN THE MAJORITY WORLD

The history of the North's apparent preoccupation with solving the problems of the Majority World through aid and intervention is littered with projects that have either failed to achieve their aims, or have created new and even worse sets of problems for local communities. Common factors include mismanagement, lack of consultation with local communities, scientific misinformation, and lack of sufficient insight into the social, political and/or ecological context.

Critics such as Arturo Escobar have argued that development policies after the Second World War became mechanisms of control that were just as pervasive as their colonial counterparts.[1] Development organisations have been accused of being caught up in their own self-perpetuation and in public relations efforts designed to create an illusion of effectiveness. In 2000, the US Congress Meltzer Commission published a report showing that 65-70 per cent of World Bank development projects in the poorest countries were failures, with no impact on alleviating poverty.[2]

We can see the recent concern with developing energy efficiency and renewable energy projects as a new phase in the history of the North's involvement in 'developing' the Majority World. The North does indeed have an important role to play in terms of having greater access to financial, technological and informational resources. There is also a clear principle of justice in terms of the North being historically responsible for the vast majority of emissions through its rapid process of industrialisation, which was in turn dependent on the extraction of vast quantities of natural resources from its various subjugated colonies in the Majority World. The great injustice of climate change is that it is the poorest parts of the world that will suffer the most from its effects, and that have contributed least to bringing it about. These historical factors contribute to the concept of 'the ecological debt', which describes the North's exploitation of the environment and natural resources of the Majority World to the advantage of some of its own populations.

Apart from providing aid to mitigate the impacts of climate change in the Majority World, one of the best ways of contributing to the payment of this debt would be for the North to invest heavily in the transition of the Majority World into low-carbon economies, while *simultaneously* investing in its own structural transition away from fossil fuels. Promoters of offset schemes (including offset schemes within the framework of the Kyoto Protocol such as the Clean Development Mechanism and Joint Implementation) argue that this is effectively what they are doing. In order to learn the lessons from decades of dubious development projects in the South, there needs to be a critical evaluation of whether the 'sustainable development' motive for creating these projects rings true, or whether they are primarily undertaken in order to provide a profitable illusion of climate action while justifying continued high emissions levels in the global North.

The motivation for developing such projects specifically in the Majority World, beneath the rhetoric of altruism and benevolence, is economic. Within the existing model of global economic inequality, there are greater financial incentives - such as export subsidies - for Northern business to execute these projects in the Majority World. These include the availability of cheap land, labour, and materials. After years of exploiting the raw materials of countries in the Majority World, we are now transforming the relatively cheap potential for the development of energy efficiency, renewable energy or carbon sequestration into a commodity that can then be sold via voluntary offset companies to consumers in the North. Here, there is a strange contradiction between the stated aim of development, and, as Oxford academic Adam Bumpus argued in a paper delivered to the Royal Geographic Society, the fact that "carbon offsets are premised on North-South inequity, you have to have a developing world if you're going to get your cheap carbon offsets."[3] Carbon offset projects appear to be simultaneously exploiting the lesser 'developed' nature of the Majority World while claiming to alleviate it.

The 'anti-politics machine'

In his 1994 work, *The Anti-Politics Machine: 'Development,' Depoliticization, and Bureaucratic Power in Lesotho*, the anthropologist James Ferguson argues that the development model effectively disempowers public debate by its reliance on a cadre of development 'experts' who evaluate and discuss projects according to the technical criteria inherent to their discipline in a way that divorces such issues from the sphere of community involvement. These experts create a set of technical criteria which restrict the sphere of legitimate criticism to that which can be specified in terms of the forms of knowledge they have created.[4] A simple analogy is that of the anti-gravity machine that appears in old science-fiction movies where gravity is suddenly suspended when it is switched on. The development apparatus, he argues, is an equivalent anti-politics machine, where even the most sensitive questions can be instantaneously de-politicised at the flick of a switch. This analysis seems as relevant as ever in this new wave of 'carbon development'.

An example of this exclusion is the offsets project being undertaken in Uganda and described in more detail in this chapter, in which community members living close to the Mount Elgon plantation said they knew nothing about the offsets credits being generated by the project. Members of the sub-county local council and top district officials were also unaware of what was going on. Residents wanted to know more about the financial benefits that the offset companies were receiving, particularly because the plantation was occupying their land, and they planned to take the matter up with their local parliamentarian.[5]

Profits will save the day

Free market theorists believe that the profit motive, unfettered by regulation and state intervention, is the only way to bring about development in the Majority World. A good example of the harmful consequences of imposing free-market based development on the Majority World has been that of water services. A report in March 2006 by the World Development Movement and the Public Services Research International Unit concludes that "the idea that private companies will find the money to deliver water and sanitation to the world's poor is a pipe dream that has led to 15 years of bad policy resulting in continuing suffering and hardship". In order to reach the UN Millennium Development Goal of halving the proportion of people without sustainable access to drinking water and basic sanitation by 2015, there would need to be an average of connecting 270, 000 people a day. Nine years of privatisation have seen only 900 people connected daily, while prices have steadily risen.[6]

What we are being asked to believe is that private, profit-led companies are best suited for developing projects to deal effectively with climate change and benefit local communities in the Majority World. Experience and studies such as the one by the World Development Movement have shown that the desire to maximise profits is often accompanied by corruption, project mis-management, deception and the neglect of the needs of local populations. The rest of this chapter will focus on three such voluntary offset projects in the Majority World where the rosy picture portrayed on the companys' websites has not lived up to the reality.

Karnataka India

"Rock Band Capitalist Tool For Cutting CO2"

The Coldplay/Carbon Neutral Company partnership has produced some of the highest profile voluntary carbon offset projects so far. The current international success of the band means that its sponsorship of a plantation of mango trees in Karnataka in Southern India has been documented on many fan sites and in the music press. Headlines in major periodicals such as *Time* magazine proclaim the project as a "Rock Band Capitalist Tool For Cutting CO2".[7] When the band made its critically acclaimed album, *A Rush of Blood to the Head* in 2002, it bought the services of the Carbon Neutral Company (CNC) to fund the planting of 10,000 mango trees by villagers in Karnataka. CNC claims that "the trees provide fruit for trade and local consumption and over their lifetime will soak up the CO2 emitted by the production and distribution of the CD".[8] Fans of the band were also encouraged to 'dedicate' a tree in the plantation. For £17.50, fans could acquire the carbon absorbing rights to a specially dedicated sapling in the forest, and get a certificate in a tastefully designed tube, with a map showing where their mango tree could be found in the Karnataka plantation.

Bill Sneyd, the Director of Operations for CNC enthusiastically described the way in which Coldplay got involved. "In offsetting the carbon emissions of their two latest albums, they specifically requested forestry projects in developing countries. At first, they were involved in a project in India, but more recently they have been involved in a forestry/community project in Mexico. And they have gotten so excited and engaged that they are talking about visiting the project after one of their upcoming tours in Mexico... It all just makes for such a superb and multi-faceted story that it draws people."[9]

In April 2006, some facets of the story emerged that were not so positive. It was reported in the *Sunday Telegraph* that many aspects of the project had been disastrous. Anandi Sharan Miele, head of the NGO Women for Sustainable Development (WSD), CNC's project partner in Karnataka, admitted that of the 8,000 saplings she had distributed, 40 per cent had died.[10] In the village of Lakshmisagara, only one person out of a village of 130 families received saplings, as the rest did not have the water resources to support them. This person was able to sustain 50 saplings out of the 150 she received due to a well she had on the land, but complained that "I was promised 2,000 rupees (£26) every year to take care of the plants and a bag of fertiliser. But I got only the saplings."[11] A number of other people from other villages told similarly disgruntled stories; "We were promised money for maintenance every year but got nothing," and "[Ms Mieli] promised us that she'd arrange the water," but the water tanker visited only twice.[12] Soumitra Ghosh from the Indian organisation North East Society for the Protection of Nature commented "It's absolutely what I expected. Most plantation projects in India end like this, after the green hype of saplings."[13]

To the casual observer, the negative impact of the project's failure may only appear to be a lot of dead mango trees. What is not so easy to assess from the reports is what the implications are for the villagers who had been led to believe that they could depend on mango harvests in future, or that they would be paid to safe-guard the carbon stored in the trees. For people as economically marginalised as these Indian villagers, a decision to have gone ahead with putting energy and resources into these mango trees could have meant forsaking some other agricultural or economic opportunity that could not be pursued after the mangos had failed.

There is a broader point here. Not only do such externally imposed and mismanaged development project fail to store carbon, but they can also have disastrous consequences for local communities. CNC may assure its clients, such as Coldplay, that it will provide them with offset credits from other projects to compensate for the mango trees' failure. But who will take responsibility for the consequences that the project failure has had for the Karnatakan villagers?

Offsetting responsibility

Part of the problem with such a project is that, while everyone would like to claim the credit for a success story, no one is willing to take responsibility for failure. Most offset companies have legal disclaimers that they are not actually able to take responsibility for their project partner's inability to fulfil projects. In this case, while Miele claims that CNC has a "condescending" attitude and that "They do it for their interests, not really for reducing emissions. They do it because it's good money," CNC claims that it funded only part of the programme and that WSD were contractually obliged to provide water and ongoing support for the plantations. A source close to Coldplay meanwhile, said that the band "signed up to the scheme in good faith with Future Forests and it's in their hands. There are loads of bands involved in this kind of thing. For a band on the road all the time, it would be difficult to monitor a forest." [14]

As of June 2006, two months after the report in the *Sunday Telegraph*, the CNC website was still selling dedicated mango trees to Coldplay fans and, as of October 2006, the plantation is still being presented as another of the company's success stories. There has been no transparency or accountability to the people who have paid to see this project realised, updating them that things were not going according to plan. In fact, as far back as 2003 the Edinburgh Centre for Carbon Management (ECCM), who act as external verifiers for CNC projects, had visited Karnataka and concluded that "WSD had been unable to make the anticipated progress with the project and had not delivered carbon payments to farmers."[15] Yet for two to three more years the CNC continued to promote and sell the project as a success story. The existence of supposedly independent verifiers like the ECCM seems to serve very little purpose if their findings are not made public and the projects continue irrespective of them.

A month after the negative allegations about the project appeared, an article promoting carbon trading in India appeared in the business section of India Today. It promoted mango plantations as "the new face of a global trade that has sprung up around controlling emission of greenhouse gases" and "a remarkable example of how innovative business ideas are not just helping to save the environment but also enrich a poorer part of the world."[16] Beside a photo of Anandi Miele smiling amidst the leaves of a mango tree, she claims that "Coldplay is not the best example today. We have gone far beyond it", citing projects she has been involved in such as the FIFA sponsorship of the Green Goal Initiative in the run-up to the Football World Cup to help 5,500 families in Karnataka build individual biogas plants.[17]

WSD is also currently working with Climate Care, whose website describes it as "an NGO in India with expertise in emissions reductions".[18] WSD wrote the initial report on the Climate Care offset scheme to build biogas digesters for villagers in the Ranthambhore National Park in Rajasthan, and is supposed to monitor the project in the long term. It remains to be seen if its involvement in this project will be as successful as the mango plantations in Karnataka.

Land rights in Uganda vs

the right to pollute in the Netherlands[19]

In 1994, a Dutch organisation called the FACE Foundation (Forests Absorbing Carbon-dioxide Emissions) signed an agreement with the Ugandan authorities to plant trees on 25,000 hectares inside Mount Elgon National Park in Uganda. Another Dutch company, GreenSeat, has been selling the supposedly sequestered carbon from the Mount Elgon plantations to people wanting to offset the emissions caused by flying. The GreenSeat website claims that just US$28 covers the costs of planting 66 trees to 'offset' the 1.32 tonnes of CO_2 emitted during a return flight from Frankfurt to Kampala.[20] Alex Muhwezi, the director of the World Conservation Union in Uganda enthusiastically described the project as "FACE gets a license to continue polluting - we get to plant some trees."[21]

A closer look at the FACE Foundation's tree planting project reveals that the project may be exacerbating complex conflicts. In Uganda, the FACE Foundation works with the Uganda Wildlife Authority (UWA), the agency responsible for managing Uganda's national parks. The UWA-FACE project involves planting a two to three kilometre-wide strip of trees just inside the 211 kilometre boundary of the National Park. According to Denis Slieker, the director of the FACE Foundation, over a third of the planned total of 25,000 hectares have already been planted.[22]

In the areas planted with trees, forest regeneration has improved, especially where the land had been used for agriculture. The project is certified under the Forest Stewardship Council (FSC) scheme as being well managed. Each year, the Société Générale de Surveillance (SGS) - the world's leading inspection, verification, testing and certification company - monitors the project to check that it complies with FSC standards. Fred Kizza, FACE's project co-ordinator in Uganda, claims that the project has improved income levels and living standards among local communities, and that the project has provided jobs, especially in planting and the tending of nurseries. The project gives out seedlings to farmers, which they plant on their farms.[23]

At first glance, it seems that Mount Elgon is providing benefits to both local communities and the national park. But a closer examination reveals serious problems that would never be apparent to the casual consumer of offsets in the Netherlands.

For a start, local council officials dispute the employment claims. They point out that most of the jobs are only available during the planting period and employ very few people. They also complain that the project has taken away what little land and income local communities had. Collecting firewood has become a serious problem and people have had to abandon the preparation of foods that take a long time to cook, such as beans.[24]

Violent evictions

In order to keep villagers out of Mount Elgon, UWA's park rangers maintain a brutal regime. In 1993 and 2002, villagers were violently evicted from the national park. Local villagers who were interviewed in 2006 claimed that since the last evictions took place, UWA's rangers have hit them, tortured them, humiliated them, shot at them, threatened them and uprooted their crops.

Denis Slieker, the director of FACE, denied that the UWA-FACE project has anything to do with these problems. He referred to an impact assessment carried out in 2001 which concluded that the main negative impacts were increased scarcity of land, reduction of access to park resources and the increase of dangerous animals. "Closer research demonstrated that the negative impacts were caused by the conversion of the area into a National Park rather than reforestation by UWA-FACE," said Slieker. "In the absence of the project people would have experienced the same impacts."[25]

The Ugandan Government did declare Mount Elgon a national park in 1993, one year before the UWA-FACE tree planting project started. But the problems associated with this decision were very much in evidence when the project started, and continue to the present day. The UWA-FACE project forms part of the management of the national park. Rather than helping solve problems relating to the national park, the FACE Foundation's tree planting is making them worse.

When the government changed the status of Mount Elgon to a national park, the people living within its boundaries lost all of their rights. According to SGS they never had any, claiming that, "the encroachers have never had legal rights to farm the land." None of the people evicted from the park have received adequate compensation. Many of the people who were evicted had nowhere to go, and many continue to farm in and around the national park.

UWA's park rangers receive paramilitary training. Park rangers actively patrol the boundary region and prevent villagers from grazing their goats and cows. David Wakikona, Member of Parliament for Manjiya County, told the Ugandan newspaper *New Vision* in 2004, "The wildlife people who operate there are very militarised, and have killed over 50 people. People feel that the Government favours animals more than the people."[26]

Masokoyi Swalikh, Mbale District Vice Chairman, points out that UWA's approach has resulted in conflicts where communities have deliberately destroyed the trees planted around the boundary. For people living around the park, the trees are a symbol of their exclusion from land that was once theirs. In 2003, local communities took action against this symbolic exclusion and in a single night destroyed a strip of eucalyptus trees over four kilometres long marking the park boundary.

In March 2002, UWA evicted several hundred more people from Mount Elgon, many of whom had lived on the land for over 40 years. Park rangers destroyed villagers' houses and cut down their crops. With nowhere to go, the evicted people were forced to move to neighbouring villages where they lived in caves and mosques.[27]

Cosia Masolo, an elder who lived in Mabembe village for over 50 years, was among those evicted in 2002. He has 20 children and now lives on a piece of land covering just one-third of a hectare. "When the UWA people came with their tree-planting activities they stopped us from getting important materials from the forest", he told Timothy Byakola in 2004. "We were stopped from going up to get *malewa* (bamboo shoots), which is a very important traditional food in the area and is a source of income. There were certain products that we used to get from the forest for the *embalu* ceremony (circumcision ritual) to be performed in the proper traditional way."[28]

In 2002, SGS stated that rehabilitation in areas where people were farming "requires the eviction of encroachers before the work can begin." SGS commented that "Mount Elgon National Park is moving in this direction", and adds that "more speed may be required to ensure the evictions are carried out successfully."[29]

Passing the buck

When questioned, Niels Korthals Altes of GreenSeat initially denied that the evictions had taken place at Mount Elgon, stating that, "That's not the case in our projects for sure."[30] When it was pointed out to him that SGS mentioned the evictions in its Public Summary, Korthals Altes said he couldn't answer specific questions on this and suggested consulting the FACE Foundation. A few days later, he acknowledged that evictions had indeed taken place, but he denied that either GreenSeat or the FACE Foundation had any responsibility. "Evicting people is not part of the UWA-FACE project," he wrote in an email. "It is a result of the government's decision to enforce the laws regarding farming in the National Park."[31]

Denis Slieker, FACE's director, was in a similar state of denial. "We carry out a reforestation project in a project area which has been assigned by the Uganda Wildlife Authority and the Ugandan government as a National Park," he said. "If for some reason there is uncertainty on that area then that needs to be solved. If the Ugandan government decides, together with the UWA, that there should be an eviction then it's their responsibility. That is not our responsibility."[32]

Slieker explained that the boundary of the tree-planting project includes a 10 metre-wide strip of eucalyptus trees. "This is designed to provide a resource that can be managed by local communities to provide pole and firewood, reducing the pressure on the park's resources," he said.[33] Although he acknowledged that people had been evicted in 1993, he claimed that, "people aren't being evicted right now."[34] He appeared to be unaware of the evictions that had taken place since the UWA-FACE project started. When researchers visited Mount Elgon in July 2006, it was obvious that the communities around the park had not seen the last of the evictions and that conflicts between local communities and UWA were ongoing.

The Benet people are indigenous to Mount Elgon. Having been evicted in 1983 and 1993, they decided to take the government to court to claim their land rights. In August 2003, with the help of a Ugandan NGO, the Uganda Land Alliance, they started proceedings against the Attorney General and UWA. The Benet accused UWA of constantly harassing them. The government meanwhile cut off all education and health services in the area and forbade the people from doing anything with the land.

In October 2005, Justice J. B. Katutsi ruled that the Benet people "are historical and indigenous inhabitants of the said areas which were declared a Wildlife Protected Area or National Park." He ruled that an area of the national park should be de-gazetted and that the Benet should be allowed to live on their land and continue farming it.[35]

The UWA-FACE project is planting trees precisely in the area of land that is disputed by local communities - the boundary of Mount Elgon National Park. The way in which the boundary is determined and by whom is a key factor in the relationship between the park management and the local communities.

In addition to the conflicts with local people around the park, the FACE Foundation (who plant the trees), and GreenSeat (who sell the offsets that pay for them), have a further problem - they cannot guarantee that the trees planted will survive. In February 2004, *New Vision* reported that the police were holding 45 people "suspected of encroaching on Mount Elgon National Park and destroying 1,700 trees" - trees planted under the UWA-FACE project.[36]

According to Slieker, this is not a problem. "Millions of trees have been planted, so a number of 1,700 is to be seen in that perspective," he said. "Of course some trees die if you plant such a large area, some trees just won't live, they'll be overtaken by other trees. That's normal in an ecosystem. That is already incorporated in the CO_2 calculation model. The model calculates the net positive benefit in carbon sequestration. We even take into account the risk of people cutting down trees. If that happens we do not get the carbon credits. It's as simple as that."[37]

But GreenSeat and FACE cannot guarantee the beneficial climatic impact of the Mount Elgon project. The only way of knowing the real impact of the project on stored carbon is by monitoring the thousands of people who have been evicted from the National Park and comparing their carbon emissions before and after the evictions. It is impossible to predict with any degree of accuracy the actions of people evicted from Mount Elgon National Park. Some of them may clear other areas of forest to continue farming. Others may overgraze the land around the park, causing soil erosion. Others may try to continue farming in the National Park. Others may move to the city and take up a higher carbon emitting lifestyle.

GreenSeat is supported in its offsetting efforts by WWF Netherlands and its customers include the Dutch House of Representatives and Senate, the Body Shop and Amnesty International. In response to questions, Ruud Bosgraaf, press officer for Amnesty International in the Netherlands, said, "We are not aware of any involvement by GreenSeat in evictions in Mount Elgon."[38] Bosgraaf is right - GreenSeat has not evicted anyone. Neither has the FACE Foundation, nor has SGS.

But on its website GreenSeat advertises its tree-planting project in Uganda to sell carbon offsets. This planting is under the management of the Mount Elgon National Park. The FACE Foundation's partner at Mount Elgon, the Ugandan Wildlife Authority, has forcibly evicted people with its military-trained rangers. If the tree planting is to continue and the company is to guarantee its offset credits, more people will be evicted.

Offsetting responsibility

Rather than offsetting carbon emissions, GreenSeat, FACE and SGS have been offsetting their own responsibility for evictions. When faced with the fact that conflict and evictions are ongoing at Mount Elgon, each of the actors involved points to one of the others, either to legitimise their own actions, or to displace responsibility. FACE Foundation doesn't blame its partner at Mount Elgon, UWA, for the evictions, but asks whether we have been in touch with IUCN, which has been working on conservation projects at Mount Elgon since 1998. IUCN in turn gives a corporate shrug of its shoulders and says that the evictions are not its responsibility.

The FACE Foundation is only one of a range of international actors that is complicit in UWA's brutal management of Mount Elgon National Park. But of all the international projects at Mount Elgon, the FACE Foundation's project is the most difficult to justify. Although there would be conflicts between the management of the national park and local communities, with or without the UWA-FACE tree planting project, the UWA-FACE project is making matters worse. If the UWA-FACE project were to be implemented in full, it would create a two to three kilometre zone around the entire national park in which villagers' rights are either eliminated or severely restricted. UWA's rangers need to guard the trees to ensure that the trees remain in place for 99 years, in accordance with the UWA-FACE contract. Meanwhile, the benefits from the trees belong to the FACE Foundation, an organisation thousands of miles away from Mount Elgon. Whether the trees are actually storing more carbon than would be the case in the absence of the project is impossible to determine. As it is, the project is contributing to villagers' problems and making a solution to those problems more difficult.

When Denis Slieker at the FACE Foundation was shown a previous article by one of the researchers critiquing their involvement in Mount Elgon, he commented, "Unfortunately the article does not show that we do whatever is in our power to improve the project, as we do with all our projects." Slieker suggested that the article should end with a solution or advice. Slieker wrote: "In general we support critical views, since it demands that we try to improve the projects constantly. We would prefer a more constructive, solution driven article, where you can be critical, but also give suggestions for solving the big issues regarding climate, deforestation and social aspects."

In terms of providing suggestions on deforestation and 'social aspects', there is an urgent need to address the land rights of the people living in and around the park. The first step towards achieving this is to acknowledge that the boundary of the national park (as well as much of the park itself) is a highly contested zone. Any top-down solution to the park boundary will result in further conflicts between park management and local people. The FACE Foundation is contributing to the tension because the carbon stored in its trees must be protected from damage from local communities already faced with conflict. Through the UWA-FACE project, the boundary of the park is being fixed, not in stone but in carbon. Rather than focussing on UWA's 'rights' to manage the national park and the 'rights' of people in the North to continue to pollute, there is an urgent need to start from the perspective of the rights of the people living in and around Mount Elgon National Park.

Energy efficient light bulbs in South Africa

South Africa is leading Africa into the new carbon world. Apart from the offset projects it hosts under the Kyoto Protocol's Clean Development Mechanism, residents in the sprawling urban township of Guguletu, Cape Town were recipients in late 2005 of ten thousand energy-efficient Compact Florescent Lightbulbs (CFLs) from Climate Care, a UK-based voluntary offset company. The idea was that Climate Care could then calculate how much emissions levels had been reduced as a result of the energy efficiency of the bulbs, and then market these hypothetical reductions back to offset consumers in the global North. Like other offset schemes, the project is symbolic of the opportunities that free market environmentalism presents to governments, business and consumers leading carbon-intensive lifestyles. Domestically, the light-bulbs scheme highlights the paradoxical relationships that the South African government has with its most vulnerable citizens and the global free market.

The first problem is that of 'additionality'. Climate Care brokered a deal with the City of Cape Town on the grounds that the project would not have been able to go ahead had it not been for the company's money. Additionality has been a contentious issue in offset projects, as it is impossible to predict the future circumstances that might arise and upset the hypothetical predictions that this additionality has been based on. In the Guguletu case, a few months after the light bulbs had been distributed, the additionality of the project was severely compromised when energy supplier Eskom implemented an enormous distribution scheme of its own. It supplied CFLs to Cape Town residents in response to a massive electricity blackout, including the residents of Guguletu. The hypothetical emissions reductions that Climate Care are selling to Northern consumers are to a large extent undermined by the fact that many of these reductions would have occurred anyway without the financial input of Climate Care.

A further challenge to additionality is that, according to Climate Care's Managing Director Tom Morton, the company only paid for the light bulbs and the reporting, not the implementation.[39] The City was made to pay for the actual distribution work done through a local energy consultancy. One of the consequences for citizens has been the loss of agency in being reduced to powerless recipients of ill-advised deals being brokered between their government and international companies like Climate Care. As is usual with offset projects in Southern countries, in having the role of "humble recipients of international charity" forced upon them, the communities were not informed as to the larger nature of the project. No one was interested in their opinions on their choice of light bulbs being used as a justification for further fossil-fuel consumption in the North.

Another consequence for these financially poor South Africans is being unwittingly complicit in the activities of the carbon world, which includes using the credits from their newly installed light bulbs to promote the interests of big corporations like British Airways and British Gas. These corporations are two of the biggest partners of Climate Care, which claims they are among the "best environmental performers". British Gas is a major CO_2 emitter through its global fossil fuel extractions. The company is currently pursuing legal action against Bolivia for taking a democratic decision to nationalise its oil resources. It is currently a partner in two large gas fields in the country and has eight exploration blocks that have not yet started production. This conflict of interest is not declared by either the company or Climate Care, casting doubt on the motivations of both companies involved in the deal. Instead, Climate Care states in its 2004 Annual Report that how companies choose to use their offsets is not an issue, proclaiming that "the climate crisis is so urgent that we should not worry about the motivation of our clients".[40] Again, we see the 'anti-politics machine' at work here, with the urgency of the climate crisis being used by Climate Care to effectively wash its hands of any of the socially or environmentally reprehensible activities that these companies might also be involved in.

The problems specifically related to the project itself revolve around the distribution of the light bulbs, which remains an area of deep contention. For starters, the ten local distributors, literally plucked from the streets of Guguletu, were given only ten days in which to hand out 10,000 bulbs.[41] This 'rush job' inevitably meant that the proper education about the use and value of the bulbs that was supposed to go in tandem with the handout was not possible. This was registered as a major complaint by the residents who were interviewed.[42] A host of other related problems emerged from the discussions. CFLs cost $2.80, more than five times the cost of traditional light bulbs. In a neighbourhood in which the monthly income is less than $135 per month (R800) replacing these bulbs is thus clearly not an option.

The other issue is that of accessibility. The big retailers that stock CFLs are not located in townships like Guguletu, which means an expensive taxi ride to the city. It would make more sense for residents to buy the cheaper counterparts at the local corner shop. This could be an argument in favour of the project, but there are other problems. The free CFLs raised expectations of more light bulbs being given. But, of the 69 low energy bulbs reported as broken from the households surveyed by Climate Care two months after the project started, none had yet been replaced. The survey, which looked at 30 per cent of the houses targeted (1131 of 3009 households) had a priority of raising awareness of energy efficiency. Perhaps a more effective educational strategy would be to inform on holistic energy saving ideas. Asmal, the Director of Environmental Affairs of Cape Town, stated that just by switching off the hot water heater when not in use, 40-60 per cent could be saved on electricity bills.[43]

Local university professor Dieter Holm[44] provided some insights on the use of the project to promote sustainable development. He believes that while there is no doubt that a project of this nature "is easy to do" and "immediately effective" in saving on domestic electricity demand, it would be more effective to introduce these bulbs at a higher level. Higher income groups are more inclined to experiment with novel technology, he argues. They also use much more electricity and that "in just one transaction you can change between 23-30 bulbs".[45] Furthermore, if such technology is introduced to lower income groups and not seen to be used by higher income users, the product becomes stigmatised - a very real possibility in the South African context. An example of this, he explains, is when solar heating was subsidised for lower income residents. In an effort to make the product cheap and accessible manufacturers made a low quality product which people ultimately rejected. The great risk with introducing CFLs in this way is that it will be considered a "poor man's [sic] version of a light bulb".

Another issue looms over Climate Care's involvement in the project. The company admitted visiting the site before the implementation of the CFL project. But even a cursory look would have revealed the problems in the neighbourhood as going much deeper than light bulbs. Context is everything. The government houses are in a poor state with faulty wiring (which does not even support the old lights), unpainted ceilings, damp walls etc. The South African government has also been criticised for its claim that these houses were meant for the poor.

But at $150 per month, when most residents earn considerably less, the costs exceed what the poor can afford. One of the residents interviewed complained, "They tried taking people out of the houses and we put them back. Even after paying the full amount asked some don't have the title deeds. We are going to court time and again. The case is still on... We are just trying to live like any other human being. We are really suffering in the new South Africa."[46]

Other questions remain over just how Climate Care expects to monitor whether the light bulbs last their stickered lifespan of 5-10 years, and how closely the energy saving gains would be measured. Despite these ambiguities, Climate Care's annual report for 2005 considers the project done and dusted. None of these concerns are presented to its clients. Morton also dismisses the criticisms levelled against his company. According to him, "Carbon offsets are a first step towards pricing carbon in our lives as well as making real reductions in the process."[47]

5 | CELEBRITIES AND CLIMATE CHANGE

Enthusiastic celebrity endorsements have fuelled the rapid rise of carbon offsets in the popular consciousness. The public fascination with celebrities means that the association of a famous name with such a scheme guarantees a certain amount of publicity and legitimacy, which in turn leads to greater investment and support for such schemes by the public. The most celebrity-obsessed newspapers and magazines are the ones least likely to offer a critical or analytical perspective on offsetting. In most cases, what we receive is a slightly paraphrased version of a press release, co-written by the offset company and the celebrity's press agent, which typically extols the virtuous, caring green credentials of the celebrity while summarising offsets as an exciting new way of dealing with climate change.

In trying to facilitate the grassroots critical mass necessary to deal effectively with climate change, there is a place for role models - public figures whose actions people are inspired to emulate. These could be well-respected community figures (teachers, religious leaders etc.) but in the current era of globalised media, they are also quite likely to be celebrities. This chapter will examine the way that celebrities have been involved in championing other causes, most notably the Live 8 concerts and the Make Poverty History campaign, and what lessons should be learnt in the light of these factors when dealing with the issue of celebrity involvement in climate change. Carbon Trade Watch also interviewed two figures in the entertainment industry about their involvement in promoting awareness of climate change and how they have chosen to directly tackle emissions rather than offset their responsibility through the likes of the Carbon Neutral Company.

How celebrity endorsement works

How do celebrity endorsements help to legitimise offsets? And why should we take what is celebrities do seriously? At the most general level, celebrity-driven politics can be treated as a symptom of the wider merger between the political and media spheres - producing new forms of 'mediatised' or 'aestheticised' politics.[1] In the face of a legitimacy crisis among democratic institutions in the global North, it can be argued, the activity of political will-formation is increasingly happening outside of these formal political spaces. Politicians themselves are responsive to this trend. From Al Gore talking climate change on *Oprah* to Tony Blair selling the Iraq war on the *Richard and Judy* show in the UK, leading politicians are as likely nowadays to accept personal interviews on chat shows as to submit themselves to interrogations on serious news shows (let alone by their parliamentary colleagues). Celebrities are in on the act too, using their status as a ticket to sit at the tables of world leaders: Bono from U2, Brad Pitt and Angelina Jolie have all been among the recent guests at the World Economic Forum in Davos, where political elites and corporate leaders meet to set the global political agenda.

The influence of celebrities is not restricted to political decision-making, however - it is also a means to achieve new legitimacy by encouraging identification with and 'trust' in the practices they promote, among which 'offsetting' is only the latest fad. At the most basic level, there is clear evidence that celebrity-endorsement is an effective means to sell products. An academic survey of books endorsed by Oprah Winfrey, for example, found that these endorsements improved their position on the best-sellers list.[2] A separate study of 110 celebrity endorsements also concluded that they have "a positive impact ... on expected future profits."[3]

Celebrity-endorsement works because what is being sold is not simply the product itself, but a way of relating to the image of that product - which is mediated through the personality of that celebrity. The anthropologist Grant McCracken argues that celebrity-endorsement involves a transfer of meaning from the product to a role embodied by the celebrity, through which an attachment and, ultimately, a desire for the product is created.[4] Such effects have also been noted in studies of celebrity endorsements of politicians and political stances - although this works better in some cases than others, depending on the familiarity and attractiveness of the celebrity concerned, and with variable effects according to the fans' existing political dispositions. In the case of carbon offsets, this process works by channeling an aspiration to do something good for the environment into a specific, marketable response - the purchase of offsets.

Such endorsements are not simply selling products, however. They also sell a certain way of relating to these products and, more importantly, of engaging with the problem of climate change. Celebrity culture in general promotes highly individualised forms of identification and social processes, and encourages forms of engagement that reduce citizenship to a set of commodity choices, as the communications scholar P David Marshall argues in his study of *Celebrity and Power*.[6] As such, it is contributing to the hollowing out of the public sphere as a potential space of deliberation. Reports of celebrities offsetting their energy usage tend to focus less on *what* these celebrities are doing than on the mere fact *that* they are doing it, which pre-empts the posing of more critical questions about endorsements itself. In this way, celebrity-driven campaigns tend to isolate carbon offsets from more considered critiques, and reduce the complex political problems they are supposed to address to individualised lifestyle solutions.

The Live 8 Fiasco

The most recent and high-profile case of celebrity involvement in progressive causes has been that of pop stars Bob Geldof and Bono's patronage of the Make Poverty History (MPH) campaign. In July of 2005, some 200,000 people flocked to Edinburgh wearing white wrist bands with the aim of putting pressure on the G8 summit to boost overseas aid, cancel completely the debts of the 62 poorest countries, set binding dates for the abolition of subsidies and other protectionist support to Northern farmers and to stop forcing liberalisation and privatisation on poor countries. In the run up to the summit, Geldof, Bono and British film director Richard Curtis announced Live 8, a series of massive pop concerts held all over the world to coincide with the summit, boasting a host of the world's biggest pop stars. From this point onwards, many within the MPH camp felt that the substance of the demands had been hijacked in favour of the showbiz glamour of the concerts. Some South African commentators drew the link from Geldof's previous attempts to solve global hunger twenty years ago. "Sir Bob's mid-1980s Live Aid famine relief strategy is widely understood to have flopped because it ignored the countervailing roles of imperial power relations, capital accumulation, unreformable global institutions and venal local elites - problems repeated and indeed amplified in Live 8."[7]

The media focus on the summit itself climaxed with Geldof's judgement on the final communiqué at a post-summit press conference. "There are no equivocations. Africa and the poor of that continent have got more from the last three days than they have ever got at any previous summit."[8] The enormous media platform that Geldof was given due to his celebrity status meant that with a few dramatic, sweeping statements in this press conference he was able to effectively whitewash the G8 and deflate the mounting critical and confrontational analysis that had been building which had called for the abolition of the summit and its neoliberal policies. It was an enormous boon in terms of high-profile political legitimacy for the summit heads of state.

Reducing issues to sound-bites

Understandably, other campaigners were furious. "People must not be fooled by the celebrities, Africa got nothing," stated Senegalese economist Demba Moussa Dembele of the African Forum on Alternatives.[9] Issa Shivji, a professor of law at the University of Dar es Salaam, stated that "The Geldof-type Live Aid Bands and musical shows assuage the conscience of the wealthy inhabitants of the North while giving political legitimacy to the military interventions and political interferences of Western leaders in the lives and affairs of the African people.... in order to make poverty history, the history of poverty must be understood."[10]

This is the key factor in terms of celebrity involvement, the fact that important analysis and context is often stripped away to leave just the media-friendly sound-bite that is then uncritically swallowed by the wider public. According to Charles Abugre, head of policy for Christian Aid, one of the organisations in the MPH coalition, "there were millions of people watching the concerts, but what was the analysis? What was the message? It was one of handouts and charity, not one of liberation defined by Africans themselves or the reality that we are actually resisting neo-colonialism and neoliberalism ourselves".[11]

The celebrity-driven approach to climate change is resulting in a similar lack of analysis, with a complex situation involving North-South relations and the ecological debt, the global inequality of energy and resource distribution and the interdependence of neoliberal economic expansion and fossil-fuel consumption reduced into a neat little gimmick whereby a small payment to a particular company absolves one of any further concern with the threat of climate change. Unfortunately, it is not that simple, and the ongoing use of celebrities to promote the pseudo-solution of offsets is delaying the shift in popular consciousness that recognises that social change is a necessary prerequisite to dealing effectively with climate change. The celebrity endorsement of offset schemes reduces the possibilities of taking action on climate change into a commodified eco-accoutrement to the glamorous showbiz lifestyle.

Positive examples of celebrity involvement

So in what ways could the high-profile nature of celebrities and those in the entertainment industry be used in a positive way to promote effective action and debate about climate change? Firstly, a high profile can be used as a platform to give more marginalised voices space to be heard. A good example of this, albeit non-climate change-related, was the work of novelist Arundhati Roy at the World Social Forum in India in 2004, where she called for a coordinated campaign against the multinational corporations that were profiting from the war on Iraq. In an article on celebrity politics, Oscar Reyes, editor of *Red Pepper* magazine, describes how she "sought to use her position to catalyse a common initiative, inviting us to 'bring our collective wisdom to bear on one single project' in a way that months of consensus meetings cannot... at the same forum, she also gave a platform to Dalit women (oppressed by the caste system) to express their grievances. This is closer to what can be achieved: celebrity as catalyst, and celebrity as facilitator, not directly voicing the concerns of others, but giving up a platform for them to do so."[2]

Celebrities and people in the entertainment industry can also lead by positive example. In terms of climate justice, this should be more about the steps that individuals have taken towards direct responsibility for aspects of their emissions intensive lifestyle rather than paying money to offset companies to absolve them of their carbon sins. For example, in January of 2006, Philip Pullman, the author of the celebrated *His Dark Materials* trilogy, announced on his blog that he was stopping flying as a means of addressing the threat of climate change.

"From now on I stay on the ground," he wrote. "This means no long-distance travel unless I can find a ship going where I want to; no flying within Europe, and certainly none inside Britain. All unnecessary. I can't think of a single reason that would make it more important for me to go to the other side of the world quickly than to save all that fuel by going slowly, or better still by not going at all. Festivals? Conferences? The days when we could thoughtlessly get on a plane and fly across the Atlantic to deliver one lecture are over. Tours to publicise a new book? Only by ship and by train."[13]

It's not just about lifestyle choices

The positive example shouldn't be restricted to individualistic lifestyle choices - there need to be more examples of celebrities who are willing to 'get their hands dirty' in actively taking part in confrontational direct action or resistance or to take prominent roles in community organising for climate-friendly societal changes like more bike lanes, affordable and improved public transport or community-based renewable energy projects. Such a celebrity is the actor Daryl Hannah, who made a name for herself through starring roles in *Splash* and *Blade Runner*. South Central, Los Angeles is a gritty, industrial wasteland that is not so far geographically from the celebrity glamour of Hollywood, but is another world in terms of poverty and social exclusion. In the midst of this, the South Central Farm was an idealistic oasis, borne out of the riots of 1992.

It grew to become the largest urban farm in the United States; 14 acres feeding over 350 (mostly migrant) families in the community. Crime dropped 70 per cent in the area and the community was thriving for 14 years. In 2003 the farm was sold to a developer without the community's knowledge and in late spring he served them an eviction notice.[14] Supporters poured into the farm, local youth set up a permanent occupation, and many celebrities joined the cause. Daryl Hannah spent several weeks in a tree-sit, used her star power to raise the issue in the mainstream media, and raised money to try to save the farm. Throughout it all, she lived amongst the farmers, participated in long, collective meetings, took her rare showers at the solar shower with the rest of the protestors, and was one of many arrested the day the bulldozers came.

Part of the problem with the endorsement of offset schemes is that it consistently emphasises the responsibility of the individual, conveniently distracting attention from the responsibility of governments and corporations. For example, it distracts from efforts to highlight the environmental injustice inherent in the fossil fuel industry - although certain celebrities are hitting back. During a fact-finding mission of the rainforests of Ecuador in 2003, Bianca Jagger sought to publicise the plight of communities affected by the oil industry:

"The purpose of my trip is to bring the attention of the world to the plight of the indigenous populations of Ecuador... ChevronTexaco's drilling practices in Ecuador constitute a crime. No developed nation should tolerate the discharge of highly toxic oil and oil by products directly into the waterways and ecosystems of their people. The Ecuadorian Courts must send a clear message that this will not be tolerated in Ecuador - that ChevronTexaco will be held accountable. We must put an end to the days where oil companies could act with total impunity in developing nations".[15]

In February 2007, Al Gore, standing alongside actress Cameron Diaz and rapper Pharrell Williams, announced Live Earth, rock concerts that would happen simultaneously around the world on 7 July 2007, including on Antarctica, to promote awareness of climate change. The organisers announced that all air travel for Live Earth artists and staff will be offset with carbon credits. Money raised from the event will go to a new foundation being created of which Al Gore is the chair. From the name, to the methodology, to the celebrities involved, the project has many parallels with 2005's Live 8. It remains to be seen whether the concert will be any less controversial in promoting a sanitised message for the masses devoid of any genuine critique or content.

Positive engagement in the entertainment industry

Carbon Trade Watch spoke to two figures in the entertainment industry about their views on offset schemes and the ways they have chosen to take responsibility for their carbon emissions. Both of these artists have not only made real adjustments in their personal and professional lives to reduce their emissions, but also engage some of the environmental and political issues surrounding climate change in the content of their work also engages. Their treatment of the issues tends to be in a creative and thought provoking, rather than a heavy-handed message of "do this" or "don't do that" or any attempt to reduce the complexity of the issues into one line slogans. Both artists highlight the fact that climate change is as much a social justice concern as it is an environmental one.

Matthew Herbert - The complexities of ethics

Matthew Herbert[16] is a musician, producer and DJ, who has produced and remixed artists as diverse as Björk, REM, John Cale, Yoko Ono and Serge Gainsbourg. Over the years, the political content of his work has become more explicit. His 2004 album, *Plat du Jour* used culinary metaphors and samples to critique not only giant food companies, but also the emissions caused by the long-distance transportation of food, body fascism, the death penalty and the war in Iraq. The sounds he sampled for his 2006 album *Scale* included coffins, petrol pumps, a tornado jet and the sound of someone being sick outside a banquet for the delegates of the notorious DSEI arms fair in London.

We asked him about his opinion on offset schemes and his personal response to climate change.

"It is hard to talk with any reasonable moral authority about ethical lifestyle choices since the boundaries of ethics are so liquid. Who leads a more ethical lifestyle: a nurse who works beyond the hours of her contract in a home for the elderly but buys everything from Tesco, or a locally-shopping vegan book publisher who ships books about ethical lifestyles by plane around the world? There are no realistic definitive answers and few moral certainties. That doesn't mean that one shouldn't take a position. Following on from the record I made about the perils and compromises of the modern food industry (*Plat Du Jour*), it seemed that there was an imperative in my own life to make it more sustainable - the most obvious one being to stop flying. That culminated in me moving to the country to grow more of my own food, generate more of my own electricity, ride my bike more and generally be healthier to myself and the planet. Depressingly though, in Brixton [London], we could walk or take public transport everywhere, whereas in the country we are much more reliant on the car.

"It has long bothered me that the embedded environmental messages in my creative work is reproduced on lumps of plastic and flown around the world. The small gesture we have made for a while is plastic-free packaging. Often with a heavy price tag to us as the producer. I am interested in digital music for its ability to be a non-polluting (apart from the electricity and the computer in the first place) system for distributing music. On these grounds, I am considering making my record label 'Accidental' a digital-only operation.

"The flying thing though is tricky. It immediately reduces my potential income enormously. It also prevents me from attending things like film premieres to films I have done music for. Not a very important event for sure, but one that is fun. So there is a politics of pleasure involved. It limits my possibilities of being exposed to new cultures, or visiting Iraq for example. It does of course mean considering travel in a different way. In the same way that the slow food movement has asked for food to be taken differently, slow travel involves taking much longer to reach places. Consequently however, it becomes economically unviable for me to travel for two months to Australia for four DJ shows. Therein lies the heart of the issue: the job I do has evolved as a direct consequence of cheap oil, polluting systems of distribution and exploitation of local resources. To simply stop it all though, offers different ethics. I now have a public voice. I have been on CNN, the BBC, Channel 4, Arte, and many international TV and radio stations talking about these exact issues. Do I stop flying to gigs in Italy, only to have half the audience fly to London to see a show I may do? The Dalai Lama still flies. So for now, I am cutting down. I am allowing myself one flight a year to America (I have family there), one to Japan (I have a business there) and one other. I'm sure I will exceed that quota but at least it's a start. Better than the 150 flights I took last year.

"As for BA and their scheme [with Climate Care], I think it smacks of the usual corporate platitudes: a simplistic and uncommitted gesture. It has the potential to cause further damage on the ground, and trees still release CO2 when they decompose. However, it's a start. Putting tax on aviation fuel would be a much better gesture. These airlines aren't bearing any of the cost of putting right any of the damage they are causing. I do however think it is an exciting start, however misguided and feeble the principle behind it, because for the first time in the history of aviation, they are publicly linking the idea of air travel with pollution, and that is a vital moment.

"The irony is, of course, that despite the best efforts of the environmental movement and various local actions around the world, the end of oil will bring about the end of cheap flights, cheap plastics, cheap motoring, cheap credit, cheap holidays, cheap consumer goods. And it will do so at an alarming pace with possibly major consequences for what we in the West call 'civilisation'. If what I've been reading is true, it seems that it has already started. Peak oil is upon us. Then all this hand-wringing will be a distant memory. It doesn't mean we should stop trying to do the right thing though."

Robert Newman - Against the Devil's orchards

Robert Newman[17] is a novelist and a stand-up comedian. In 1993, he was part of a duo that became the first comedy act to perform sell-out dates at Wembley Arena. Since that time his work has become more politically influenced, and he has participated in many different ways in actions and mobilisations in the UK. His most recent stand-up routine, *No Planet B - The History of the World Backwards* wittily documents the rise of our addiction to oil by portraying the flow of time in reverse, culminating in the historic capping of the final oil-well in Pennsylvania in 1859, thus bringing to an end the hydro-carbon era. His televised routine *The History of Oil* encompassed subjects such as petrol geo-politics and peak-oil, and the electricity for the live show was provided by members of the audience pedaling bicycle-powered generators.

Carbon Trade Watch: Can you talk a little bit about the decisions you have made about your patterns of energy consumption with regards to climate change?

Robert Newman: I don't fly short-haul, i.e. anywhere in Europe, I don't own a car, I am with Good Energy [a UK-based renewable energy provider] and on Tuesday a man is coming round to fit double-glazing. Here's an embarrassing admission: I probably would never have got round to getting double-glazing if I hadn't bought a new settee which only fits next to a really draughty window. I cycle and use the tube. I try never to go to supermarkets. I don't eat fruit out of season unless I've recently been chucked, in which case I persuade myself that the Argentinian blueberries came by sailboat.

CTW: What prompted you to make these decisions? What impact have they had on your personal or professional life?

RN: A friend was round for dinner in my back garden one night three years ago he used the phrase "There's no excuse for flying short-haul" in relation to someone else. And that was that for me. All I needed was for someone to say it with certainty.

The next year I did a 26-city tour of USA. This tested my resolve. I did 36 hour train rides (which necessitated my giving up smoking before the trip - a hidden bonus). I was able to tour very cheaply because I had an Amtrak one-month pass which let me go on any train for a month for about $300. It made the journey more of a journey and I felt I really knew the country when I got back. And I'd met some people who weren't executives. But I did fly rather than spend five hours overnight in Chicago bus stop or take three days to get from Montreal to New Orleans.

CTW: British Airways have teamed up with Climate Care to create a scheme where you can pay money to offset the emissions from your flight. Would you be tempted to keep flying as you did before but use this scheme to offset your emissions, and if not, why not? What's your opinion on this partnership between BA and Climate Care?

RN: First of all, there is not enough money in the world to offset the emissions from flying. Even if you combined all the treasuries and gold reserves and assets and security bonds of every country in the world, how much, for example, will it cost to put Bangladesh on stilts? What daily-rate were you thinking of paying the workers who are carrying ice and snow back up to the top of Kilimanjaro? How many laboratories with how many tenured research fellows and professors before we fine-tune the gamma-ray that's going to zap the ice-crystal clouds in the upper troposphere caused by vapour trails?

Second, what you are paying for is not to offset emissions but to offset the danger of regulation or full-cost accounting being imposed on BA. Who or what are Climate Care? Where did they come from? The solution to this problem is the grounding of the air-fleet except for air ambulances and using the

CTW: Some artists like the Rolling Stones, Coldplay and KT Tunstall have chosen to pay money to the Carbon Neutral Company (formerly Future Forests) to make their tours or albums 'carbon neutral'. What do you understand by the term carbon neutral?

RN: This leaves me with some questions. I wonder how tough and Elliot Ness-like are the Carbon Neutral Company are around the Stones? Do they swoop unannounced? Who's doing the sums? Who says it's carbon neutral? Does carbon neutral include all the merchandise, all the stadium's electricity, all the paper cups, all the people driving cars to the gigs, all the millions of CDs and DVDs pressed and freighted from Zhengzhou Province or Baluchistan or Solihull to all the brightly burning high street megastores?

Also some of these plantations people talk about are what the Amazonian U'wa people call 'Devil's Orchards' (quite rock 'n' roll really!): single species stands of trees with no understorey or biodiversity.

6 I POSITIVE RESPONSES TO CLIMATE CHANGE

In the preceding chapters, it has been shown that:

* Offset companies are selling 'peace of mind' to consumers where none should exist as regards climate change, and that this breeds complacency.
* Some of the most polluting companies (and politicians) are using offsets as a cheap form of greenwash, as a distraction from their inherently unsustainable practices and refusal to take more serious action on climate change.
* Creative accountancy and dubious scientific methodologies are often used to inflate profit margins.
* Our knowledge of the carbon cycle is so limited that it is impossible to say whether plantations even have even a net positive benefit in terms of mitigating climate change, let alone exactly quantifying this supposed benefit into a sellable commodity.
* It is impossible to accurately determine a hypothetical baseline of what would have happened if the project had not taken place that would enable one to calculate how many sellable credits have been generated.
* Projects that look great on the website or in the leaflet are often, in practice, mismanaged, ineffective or detrimental to the local communities who have to endure them.
* The media and certain celebrities have been complicit in promoting an analysis of climate change that puts all the focus on individual lifestyles and draws attention from the wider, systemic changes that need to be made in our societies and economies.

In January 2007 the British government announced a set of standards to which companies offering offset services should adhere, in response to increasing criticisms of the offsets industry.[1] The standard put forward was that companies should only use carbon credits that had been certified under the methodology for generating project-based credits under the Kyoto Protocol, through the Clean Development Mechanism (CDM) and Joint Implementation (JI). The ministers involved argued that this would give the projects more scrutiny and ensure that consumers were buying genuine emissions reductions rather than 'hot air'.

There are a number of reasons why these proposed standards are ineffective. For a start, it is entirely voluntary. Yet the experience of self-regulation in other sectors is, generally, that it does not work and moreover is a tool to pre-empt proper and legally enforceable requirements.

Secondly, this voluntary standard does nothing to address the fact that offsets are being falsely sold as a legitimate means of taking action on climate change. Douglas Alexander, the UK Government's Transport Secretary said that the proposed standards will "encourage many more people to consider how they can lighten the footprint they leave on the planet," while David Miliband, the Environment Minister, commented that "people need to be sure that the way they offset is actually making a difference."[2]

Thirdly, the methodology for verifying Clean Development Mechanism (CDM) projects under Kyoto has been beset with numerous allegations of corruption, project mismanagement, lack of verifiable reductions and negative impacts on local communities. Some chemical factories in China have been generating billions of Euros in CDM credits by installing cheap equipment that stops the generation of a potent greenhouse gas called HFC-23. In a report in the January 2007 issue of *Nature* magazine, it is estimated that it would have cost €100 million to make these changes by simply regulating the implementation of the equipment through an international process or through international funding, but instead €4.6 billion has been spent on purchasing the massive amounts of credits generated by the CDM projects.[3] This is Kyoto-generated money that could have been invested in renewable energy projects, but has instead gone to the owners of the chemical factories, who are able to use the money to invest in more polluting factories. China has become the largest exporter of CDM credits through the HFC-23 loophole, so there is a good chance that if you were to buy certified credits from an offset company, you would be supporting this sort of industrial endeavour.

There is increasing evidence that CDM projects are not working, and we have documented this elsewhere in a study jointly published by the Transnational institute and the University of KwaZulu-Natal in South Africa, *Trouble in the Air - Global Warming and the Privatised Atmosphere*, which provides rich empirical detail about the fraudulence and injustice of various projects planned for South Africa under the CDM.[4]

So if neither the certified nor the voluntary market can be relied upon for purchasing emissions reductions, the question remains as to how people should take action on climate change. In debating about offsets, time and time again the argument is put forward that they are 'better than nothing' or 'a good first step.' People who are against offsets are portrayed as 'militant greens' who advocate extreme measures that are beyond the reach of 'normal' people.

To ask what is the alternative to offsets is to give them a sort of legitimacy that they do not deserve. Genuine climate change action has been going on for a long time before offsets ever appeared on the scene, and will go on for a long time after they have eventually been dismissed as exploitative free-market gimmickry. To pose 'doing nothing about climate change' against offsetting is a false opposition. It is more a question of choosing from the rich array of effective and empowering opportunities that there are to take action while ignoring bogus 'solutions' like offsets from the very outset.

A sizeable proportion of any sum given to an offset company is automatically swallowed up by intermediaries, with the money going to external verifiers, number crunchers, marketing people, project consultants and executive salaries. This is only one of the reasons that money spent purchasing credits is extremely ineffective. After making all the energy-efficiency and emissions reducing changes possible, companies and individuals would be much better off directly supporting initiatives that try to influence the way that the remaining energy requirements are generated, cutting out the dubious number crunching and the related 'offset' greenwash.

Effective climate action starts with addressing the fact that big cuts need to be made in the disproporationate share of emissions that the North is responsible for, and recognising that it also controls a disproportionate share of global wealth and technological resources. These should be shared if the North is to support the development of the low-carbon economy in the South in a non-colonialist fashion.

There are many different forms that this support could take, for individuals, institutions and even companies that are themselves locked into the logic of the market. Based in London, Alexanders is a removals and storage service with a strong environmental mission statement which promotes resource efficiency as part of its daily work (such as using crates instead of cardboard boxes and using recycled packaging materials) as well as promoting energy conservation in the office and using scrap paper and double sided printing.[5] They also choose to "invest in renewable energy projects around the world, enabling businesses in under-developed countries to run more energy efficiently, thus reducing the overall impact on our environment".[6] Nowhere on the website does this suggest that this investment is somehow intended as some sort of compensation for their unavoidable emissions as part of their work. This investment is simply one part of a well-rounded plan to taking action on climate action.

What is even more impressive is that the company has a healthy commitment to "keep up to date with all research relating to environmentally friendly projects to endeavour to steer clear of those which may not be as beneficial to the environment as they seem."[7] Rather than blithely giving money away to the first organisation with an impressive looking website and a flashy display of marketed green credentials, the company claims to take an active and critical perspective on how it is choosing to spend its money so as to make sure that it does so wisely.

Samantha Pope, one of the directors at Alexanders, said that when investigating their company's environmental policy "our research led us directly to carbon offset schemes, where we would become 'carbon neutral' by investing money in projects which would offset our own carbon emissions. However, through further investigation we realized that we weren't comfortable with this concept - that it was very easy to feel as though our company's carbon emissions could be 'neutralised' through our contributions, diverting our attention away from being more conscious of reducing our impact on the environment at source. We also wanted to find a project that would receive most, if not all, of our donation - something which is possible with the Border Green Energy Team (BGET) but which was impossible through carbon offset schemes."[8]

This critical research has lead Alexanders to financially support the work that BGET is doing in South East Asia. Chris Greacen, who works with BGET says that he thinks "that this alternative to carbon offsets is a great way to help fund organisations like ours that are aren't involved in carbon trading shell games, and are making a difference on the ground in terms of shaping the future of energy infrastructure to be cleaner and more democratic."[9]

In Thailand, the Palang Thai organisation, which is a part of BGET, works to ensure that "the transformations that occur in the Mekong region's energy sector are economically rational, and that they augment, rather than undermine, social and environmental justice and sustainability".[10] In 2002 the group drafted legislation enacted by the Thai government that requires utilities to allow interconnection of renewable energy generators, with the result that dozens of projects are now connected and selling over 16 MW of renewable energy under the programme. Earlier, an analysis conducted by Palang Thai played a key role in a successful campaign that led to the cancellation of two planned coal-fired power plants. In 2005 they worked with consumer groups to successfully reverse the illegal privatisation of the state monopoly utility EGAT. They are currently working on a package of Thai power sector reforms that will include an independent regulatory authority and reforms to the planning process so that inexpensive, clean options like demand side management,[11] combined heat and power,[12] and low-cost biomass-fuelled electricity generation can no longer be systematically ignored.

Border Green Energy Team (BGET) is a collaborative project involving Palang Thai that deals directly with communities.[13] On a minimal budget, BGET provides hands-on appropriate technology training and financial support to village innovators in renewable energy in ethnic minority areas on both sides of the Thai/Burma border. It has worked with communities to build micro-hydro projects that serve hundreds of homes, installed renewable energy infrastructures in the refugee camps along the border and provided training in their maintenance, and provided renewable energy systems and training to local medics and clinics who tend to many of the hundreds of thousands of people caught in the cross fire of the civil war in Burma.

Unlike purchasing offset credits, the money that has been sent will go in its entirety to the project, there are no complex and falsified calculations of hypothetical emissions cuts that will happen by the additional capacity of BGET to pursue its objectives, and no one is under the illusion that the emissions that Alexanders are responsible for in England have magically disappeared. One of the most important distinctions however is the fact that the project is being supported as a good thing in its own right rather than as an adjunct to any kind of plan involving Northern countries dealing with their own emissions. There are enormous possibilities for support and learning in *both* directions between countries in the North and South in the transition towards low-carbon economies, and these need not be based on the neo-colonialist assumption that support for projects in the South is conditional upon the ability of a global economic elite to maintain higher emissions levels.

It's not just about the money - The Ogoni struggle

It is equally important to stress that taking climate action isn't just about the money. Even if the vast majority of individuals and companies were to provide some sort of financial assistance to progressive and effective climate related projects in this way, the underlying economic and political structures which depends on such levels of fossil-fuel consumption to sustain itself, will remain relatively untouched. The most efficient way to bring about more profound change is through collective action and political organising.

The act of commodification at the heart of offset schemes assigns a financial value to the impetus that someone may feel to take climate action, and neatly transforms this potential to bring about change into another market transaction. There is then no urgent need for people to question the underlying assumptions about the nature of the social and economic structures that brought about climate change in the first place. One just has to click and pay the assigned price to get 'experts' to take action on your behalf. Not only is it ineffective and based on half-baked guessing games and dubious science, it is also very disempowering for the participants.

The single most effective - and incontrovertible - way of dealing with climate change is drastically to limit the quantity of fossil fuels being extracted. Providing support for communities who are resisting the efforts of the industries to extract and burn ever-increasing quantities, therefore, is one of the most important strategies in dealing with climate change. Yet it is the least encouraged because, unlike carbon offsets, it involves posing a critical challenge to the established systems of corporate power and societal organisation.

Around the world, countless communities and grassroots organisations are mobilising against the governments and industries that are ignoring the environmental and social justice costs of maintaining the carbon-intensive global economy. One of the most inspirational examples of this resistance in recent times has been the successful resistance of women from the Ogoni tribe of Nigeria against the petrol multinational Shell. The extraction of oil usually involves the extraction of natural gas as a by-product. In the North, this gas is usually used to create electricity or petrochemicals, but in Nigeria in order to cut costs, Shell was simply flaring the gas - burning it off into the atmosphere. In June 2005, the Port Harcourt organisation, Environmental Rights Action stated that "More gas is flared in Nigeria than anywhere else in the world. Estimates are notoriously unreliable, but roughly 2.5 billion cubic feet of gas associated with crude oil is wasted in this way everyday. This is equal to 40 per cent of all Africa's natural gas consumption in 2001, while the annual financial loss to Nigeria is about US $2.5 billion. The flares have contributed more greenhouse gases than all of sub-Saharan Africa combined. And the flares contain a cocktail of toxins that affect the health and livelihood of local communities, exposing Niger Delta residents to an increased risk of premature deaths, child respiratory illnesses, asthma and cancer."[14]

After the execution of Ken Saro-Wiwa and eight other Nigerian anti-Shell activists in what was described by a senior British barrister as "an act of state-sponsored murder" in 1995, women from the Ogoni villages spearheaded a remarkable campaign to stop the flaring from taking place. The Nigerian women mobilised people from the many different ethnic communities of the region, used direct action and political pressure in pursuit of their aims and endured a violent, repressive militarisation of the area as a result, including rape and murder. In 2005, some of the Ogoni women's groups involved were labelled as 'terrorists' by the government, using the discourse of the 'war on terror' to maintain the legitimacy of the fossil-fuel corporation.

The essay, "Climate Change and Nigerian Women's Gift to Humanity" describes how the campaign, "publicised the explicit connections between the destruction of the Africans' economy and the destruction of the global ecosystem by Shell's persistent practice of burning off associated natural gas. Nigerian peasant women asked for solidarity from women and other international activists in a joint campaign to protect life by putting a stop to the depredations of Big Oil."[15]

An important part of the campaign, although obviously secondary to the struggle of the Ogoni women themselves, was the international solidarity that was shown from civil society groups, ranging from the more established NGOs to the autonomous direct action group in London in 1999 who occupied the Shell Headquarters and "barricaded themselves in the Managing Directors' offices and broadcast the event to the outside world via digital cameras, lap-top computers and mobile phones. Six hours later, police cut off electricity, smashed down the wall and arrested the activists."[16]

In January 2006, Nigerian courts ordered Shell to stop the flaring of natural gas. In September 2006 a Nigerian newspaper stated that the oil giant's license over the Ogoniland was going to be revoked due to its inactivity over the previous decade, as the fierce resistance of the Ogoni people had made it impossible for it to operate there since 1993.[17] The Ogoni people, at enormous cost to themselves, their lands, their livelihoods, had won.

It isn't possible, without reverting to the esoteric accounting procedures of the offset companies, to quantify how large the emissions reductions have been as a result of the social justice struggle of the Ogoni women in shutting down the largest source of greenhouse gases in Sub-Saharan Africa. Under the absurd logic of the offsets market, it would be quite appropriate for the Ogoni women to start marketing the emissions that have been avoided as a commodity to the polluters and consumers in the North. However, as Larry Lohmann argues in his book *Carbon Trading*, "carbon credits go to well-financed, high-polluting operations capable of hiring professional validators of counterfactual scenarios. They do not go to non-professional actors in already low-emitting contexts or social movements actively working to reduce use of fossil fuels."[18]

The carbon cop-out

The hard-won victory of the Ogoni women, a huge success in terms of both social justice and climate change, depended on community empowerment, confrontational politics and international solidarity. One of the most distressing effects of the culture of offsets is the fact that it negates all three of these factors. Instead of community empowerment, climate change is presented as a matter of individualistic morality and lifestyle choices that discourages collective political action. We are being led to believe that responsible consumer choice is all that is necessary on our parts rather than engaging in a different kind of political responsibility and activity that confronts the fact that there are profound changes that need to be made in our society in order to effectively deal with climate change. The notion of international solidarity is commodified by carbon offsets, transformed into a one-sided affair in which a neo-colonial relationship of economic advantage and conditional aid is established. When the Ogoni women of Nigeria appealed to the world to support their struggle, they appealed primarily for international political action rather than financial assistance. It is beyond the scope of any offsets scheme to support this sort of social change that is so necessary in the face of climate change.

Individual, institutional, political and social responses to climate change are taking place all over the globe. The question of how much we can limit the damage caused by climate change depends on the effectiveness of these responses and how exponentially they can multiply. The effectiveness of these models should always be tempered by assessing success from a social justice perspective. For example, carbon taxation might be a very useful tool in reducing emissions, as long as one is very alert to how this might disproportionately impact the money-poor. The concept of the 'just transition' to the low-carbon economy provides a framework for being mindful that the impacts of the transition are shouldered as equitably as possible.

Promoting a more systemic approach to climate change would not seek to reduce the problem to marketing gimmicks, celebrity endorsements, technological quick-fixes, or neo-colonial exploitation. Any individual, organisation or government embracing this holistic attitude would commit to doing everything they could to reduce their climate impact, but would not offset responsibility for any of their remaining emissions. Rather they would commit to demanding, adopting and supporting climate policies that reduce emissions at source as opposed to offsets or trading. They would support stricter regulation and oversight and penalties for polluters on community, local, national and international levels, and they would commit to supporting communities adversely impacted by climate change and so-called 'climate-friendly' projects. Finally they would endorse the notion that real solutions to climate change require social change and they would count themselves to be a part of that movement, spending time and energy towards achieving such change.

APPENDIX -

OFFSETS AND 'FUTURE VALUE ACCOUNTING'

Jamie Hartzell

We often hear offset companies talking about how we can offset our personal emissions. But what is the main aim of offsetting? It is to reduce our carbon emissions to zero.

The Carbon Neutral Company calls this being carbon neutral. Climate Care says we can be climate neutral. But if you look at the websites of Climate Care or the Carbon Neutral Company you won't find the terms carbon neutral or climate neutral defined. They leave that to our intuition. So what do we think these terms actually mean?

We can say then that intuitively carbon or climate neutral means that the same amount of carbon that we cause to emit is offset through carbon reduction or absorption projects such as tree planting, energy efficiency or renewable energy generation projects. We could say that our carbon emissions and our carbon offsets are 'in balance'. Our carbon budget, or our carbon balance, is zero.

But this definition ignores one key question: over what time frame does the amount of carbon emitted have to be fully offset for our carbon balance to be zero?

Let me present a few possible views on the acceptability of different time frames:

1. The life of a tree is 100 years, so I am happy if my emissions are offset in that time frame
2. I'd want to see all my emissions offset in 20 years, by 2026
3. My emissions should be reduced by 20 per cent by 2012, in line with UK government targets
4. All my emissions should be offset within one year
5. All my emissions should be offset before the next time I fly
6. If it takes 5 hours to fly London New York, my emissions should be offset by the time I arrive.

Which of these are acceptable? And which would still legitimately allow the use of the term carbon neutral? To say that emissions have to be offset before a plane lands seems quite extreme. But equally, to take 100 years to offset our emissions does not seem acceptable, when global temperatures are set to rise several degrees and a large percentage of the world will be underwater in that time.

In fact, the speed with which we need to offset our emissions depends on two things:

First it depends on the impending nature of the climate crisis. Just how fast do we need to reduce our emissions to stop global warming?

Second, it depends on the rate at which global carbon dioxide emissions continue to rise. If emissions continue to go up, we need to offset even faster to meet reduction targets.

Ploughing through the websites of the different offset companies, it is virtually impossible to see how they are treating the time issue. They are clearly making assumptions about how many years the carbon saved will operate over, and so how much carbon will in the end be saved, but these assumptions are not published.

Climate Care offers three ways to offset your emissions - through energy efficiency projects, which make up 50 per cent of total carbon savings, renewable energy projects, which give 20 per cent of carbon savings, and tree planting, which gives the remaining 30 per cent.

From information gleaned from the annual report and website and through conversations with Tom Hinton, MD of Climate Care, I estimate that Climate Care calculates its emission reductions over approximately the following periods:

Type of Project	Years to offset emissions	Basis on which calculated	% of all offsets
Energy efficiency	6 years	Life of low energy light bulb	50%
Renewable energy	12 years	Life of wind turbine	20%
Tree planting	100 years	Life of tree	30%

With this information it is possible to calculate how long it takes to offset carbon through Climate Care. Let's take an example.

Say I flew to New York one way, on New Year's Eve 2005. According to Climate Care, this will result in the emission of 0.77 tonnes of carbon dioxide, which I can offset for £5.77, with the money I give them being spent on the range of projects listed above.

Over time, my carbon balance will then look like this:

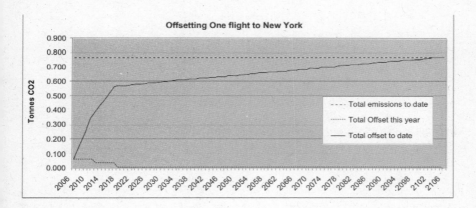

You can see that by 2018, 12 years after I took the flight, my original emissions are 80 per cent offset. Six years of energy efficiency savings and 12 years of renewable energy generation are having their effect. But then things don't look so good. Because the tree projects are only offsetting my emissions at the rate of 0.3 per cent of my original emissions a year, it actually takes till 2106 before my emissions are completely neutralised. That's 100 years. What will be the state of the climate crisis by then?

But of course Climate Care isn't just claiming you can offset one flight and still be climate neutral. Their idea is that even if you fly every year, so long as you offset you will remain climate neutral. How true is this? Let's assume that I fly to New York and back again, every New Year's Eve for the next 30 years, and faithfully pay my £5.77 each time.

Using the same basis of calculation, my carbon budget now looks like this:

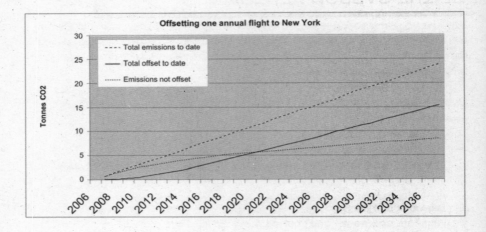

Of course as I fly every year, my total emissions are steadily rising year on year, as shown by the dashed line. As I pay money to Climate Care every year, my offsets are also rising, as shown by the dark continuous line.

But my offsets are not rising as fast as my emissions, as they occur over a much longer time frame. And so, as the dotted line shows, my total emissions not offset are rising.

So not only is my position far from climate neutral, quite the opposite is true. Each time I fly, the carbon in the atmosphere increases. My carbon balance is going in the wrong direction.

Let's say I am a more frequent flyer. I take not one but three return flights to New York a year for 30 years. Is it harder for me to offset my emissions? Assuming I pay the £5.77 per flight Climate Care asks of me, my carbon balance then looks like this:

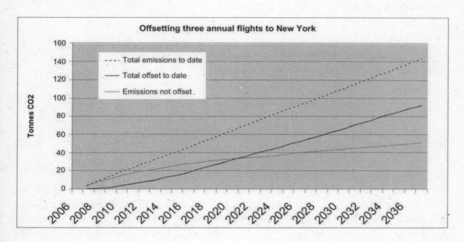

The pattern is much the same, but the numbers are bigger. When I flew only once a year, by 2036 I was left with a 'negative balance' of 8.5 tonnes of CO2 that I hadn't managed to offset. When I fly six times as often, by 2036 I'm left with a staggering 51 tonnes of CO2 that I haven't offset. In each case that is 11 years of emissions that haven't been offset.

But the point is that when I fly more often, I am even less climate neutral. Flying more frequently means that I need to do more offsetting to have any hope of achieving climate neutrality.

So the idea of achieving climate neutrality through offsetting is no more than media spin. First, it takes 100 years to fully cancel out the carbon effect of one aeroplane flight. Second, the more you fly, the more you need to offset, and finally, depending on how quickly you think offsetting needs to happen, it is also more expensive to offset than Climate Care would lead us to believe.

How much should we be paying to offset? Let's go back to the original table of offset time objectives. How much should we be paying to Climate Care if we want to achieve our objectives:

Timespan to offset emissions	Cost of offsetting a flight to New York
In 100 years (Life span of tree)	£5.77
In 20 years, by 2026	£10
20% reduction by 2010, in accordance UK Government targets	£20
Within one year	£50
Before I fly again (3 flights a year)	£200
By the time my flight arrives	£86,402

So what can we conclude?

First, we are told that offsetting makes us climate neutral when it doesn't. Each time we fly, our emissions go up.

Second, offsetting is far too cheap. Depending on how quickly we think we need to offset, we need to be paying as much as 15,000 times more to see our emissions offset in a sensible time frame. The question remains if a company like Climate Care could even develop schemes fast enough to achieve this level of offsetting.

In a recent *New Internationalist* article, the founder of Climate Care Mike Mason was quoted as saying "I would rather that 100 per cent of people offset their emissions from flights than 50 per cent of those people not fly at all."

But if this were to happen, by Climate Care's own calculations, it would be 2020 before offsetting was achieving the same level of saving as a straight 50 per cent cut in flights. It's up to Mike to decide if he is willing to wait that long.

The reason why the offset companies can argue for carbon neutrality is they are using a carbon calculation method that is best termed 'future value accounting'. Carbon savings expected to be made in the future are counted as savings made in the present. This is the same technique used by Enron to inflate its profits - and sooner or later I expect, just like Enron, the house of cards will come tumbling down.

However I fear the technique of using "future value carbon accounting" may run much deeper than just the small schemes run by voluntary offset companies. They may also apply to the Clean Development Mechanism of the Kyoto

Protocol. This is the mechanism by which developed nations invest in the less developed to achieve future carbon savings, allowing them to then emit more carbon themselves.

The UK is looking to achieve two thirds of its carbon emissions reductions through this mechanism. But if this is done through 'future value carbon accounting', it will not be just a few carbon offset companies that come crashing down, it will be international climate negotiations.

NOTES

Introduction

[1] The concept and practice had been established for quite some time already in the Islamic world

[2] E Doogue, "Catholics and Protestants Discuss Indulgences," *Christianity Today*, 26 February 2001, www.christianitytoday.com/ct/2001/109/45.0.html

[3] D Adam, "Can planting trees really give you a clear carbon conscience?," *The Guardian*, 7 October 2006, http://environment.guardian.co.uk/climate-change/story/0,,1889830,00.html

[4] D Adam, "You feel better, but is your carbon offset just hot air?," *The Guardian*, 7 October 2006, www.guardian.co.uk/frontpage/story/0,,1889790,00.html

[5] "Carbon Management & Carbon Neutrality in the FTSE All-Share," Standard Life Investments, July 2006

Chapter 1: Corrupting the Climate Change Debate

[1] R Heinberg, "The Party's Over: Oil, War and the Fate of Industrial Societies," Clairview books, 2005

[2] *ibid*

[3] N Watt, "Carry on flying, says Blair - science will save the planet," *The Guardian*, January 9, 2007

[4] D Adam, "Can planting trees really give you a clear carbon conscience?," *The Guardian*, 7 October 2006

[5] from the Climate Friendly website, http://climatefriendly.com/

[6] from the Carbon Clear website, www.carbon-clear.com/what_we_do.htm

[7] "Greenwash derives from the term whitewash and indicates that organisations using greenwash are trying to cover up environmentally and/or socially damaging activities, sometimes just with rhetoric, sometimes with minor or superficial environmental reforms." From International Encyclopedia of Environmental Politics, edited by John Barry and E. Gene Frankland, Routledge, London, 2001.

[8] "Carbon Offset Scheme Launched," DEFRA Press Release, 12 September 2005, www.defra.gov.uk/news/2005/050912b.htm

[9] "BA Profits Up by 20%," 24 May 2006, from the Business Travel Europe website

[10] E Addkey, "Boom in Green Holidays as Ethical Travel Takes Off," *The Guardian*, 17 July 2006

[11] from the Terrapass website, www.terrapass.com

[12] from the Climate Care website,

[13] Dr. P Wells, "Offroad Cars, Onroad Menace," Greenpeace UK, 31 March 2006

[14] from the Jumpstart Ford website, http://jumpstartford.com/why_ford/

[15] from the BP website, www.bp.com.au/globalchoice/faq.asp#n

[16] from the Backpacker Campervan Rentals website, www.backpackercamper-vans.com/cheap-campervans/1213/THL+BP+Global+Choice.aspx

[17] G Johnson, "US: Greenwashing Leaves a Stain of Distortion; Ford's Hybrid Electric SUV," *LA Times*, 22 August 2004, http://corpwatch.live.radicaldesigns.org/article.php?id=11505

[18] D Biello, "Climate Friendly Fuels?" from *Ecosystem Marketplace*, www.greenbiz.com/news/reviews_third.cfm?NewsID=28097

[19] ibid

[20] P Huck, "Burning Questions," *The Guardian*, 23 August, 2006

[21] M Tran, "BP revs up for Carbon Neutral Monitoring," *The Guardian*, 23 August 2006

Chapter 2: The Rise and Fall of Future Forests

[1] A Ma'anit, "If You Go Down to the Woods Today," *New Internationalist*, July 2006

[2] C Jones, "Will you plant enough trees to save the world this year?," *The Evening Standard*, 16 June 2003

[3] "The Rolling Stones' concerts go environmental," *The Sunday Telegraph*, 24 August 2003

[4] J Hodgson, "Paint it Green: Stones' concerts are a gas," *The Sunday Observer*, 24 August 2003

[5] from the Carbon Neutral Company website, www.carbonneutral.com/coldplay/

[6] from the Carbon Neutral Company website, www.carbonneutral.com/shop/results.asp?cat1=Celebrity%20Promotions

[7] Press Release "Environmentalists Cry Foul at Rock Stars' Polluting Companies' Carbon Neutral Claims,' May 2004, www.sinkswatch.org/pubs/Environmentalists%20cry%20foul.pdf

[8] Future Forests Carbon Sequestration Agreement, Coatham Wood, 26 September, 2001

[9] M Chittenden, "Rock stars' green trees may be hot air," *The Sunday Times*, 29 January 2006

[10] "Plant your own trees - don't pay others to do it for you," 13 April 2005, www.off-grid.net/index.php?p=365

[11] downloadable from www.hie.co.uk/Default.aspx.LocID-0fihiesv3005006.faq_id-191.htm

[12] assuming 1,000 trees per hectare - according to the Carbon Neutral Company website, which said "If you are buying on a tree-by-tree basis, then our planting partners plant and maintain enough saplings to make sure that there is at least one for you at the 5-year mark - in the UK this corresponds to at least 1,100 saplings per hectare, which is the minimum amount recommended by the UK Forestry Commission to yield a healthy woodland."

[13] "The Rolling Stones Gather No Gas as they come clean into Scotland," 17 September 2003, www.rollingstones.com/news/article.php?uid=103

[14] from the Carbon Neutral Company website

[15] D Biello, "Speaking For The Trees - Voluntary Markets Help Expand the Reach of Climate Efforts," *Environmental Finance*, 14 September 2005

[16] *ibid*

Chapter 3: The problems with trees and light bulbs

[1] A Jha, "Global Warming: Blame the Forests," *The Guardian*, 12 January 2006

[2] A Jha, "Planting trees to save planet is pointless, say ecologists," *The Guardian*, 15 Dec 2006

[3] D Adam, "Can planting trees really give you a clear carbon conscience?," *The Guardian*, 7 October 2006

[4] S Bond, "Energy Firm Rapped Over Carbon Offset Claims," EDIE News Centre, 11 October 2006, http://www.edie.net/news/news_story.asp?id=12114&channel=0#

[5] The Carbon Neutral Company FAQs, www.carbonneutral.com/pages/faqs.asp

[6] G Simmonds, Letter to the Editor, *The Sunday Telegraph*, 21 September 2003, www.telegraph.co.uk/opinion/main.jhtml?xml=/opinion/2003/09/21/dt2105.xml

[7] L Lohmann, "Carbon Trading: A Critical Conversation on Climate Change, Privatisation and Power," *Development Dialogue* no.48, September 2006

[8] see for instance, "Avoiding Dangerous Climate Change," edited by H J Schellnhuber, *The Cambridge University Press*, Feb 2006

[9] "Carbon Offset - No Magic Solution to Neutralise Fossil Fuel Emissions," FERN Briefing Note, June 2005, www.fern.org/media/documents/document_884_885.pdf

[10] D Adam, "Can planting trees really give you a clear carbon conscience?," *The Guardian*, 7 October 2006

[11] L Lohmann, "Trading: A Critical Conversation on Climate Change, Privatisation and Power," *Development Dialogue* no.48, September 2006

[12] *ibid*

[13] M Grubb et al. "The Kyoto Protocol: A Guide and Assessment", Royal Institute for International Affairs, London, 1999

[14] M Trexler, "A Stastically driven approach to offset-based GHG additionality determinations: What can we learn?", *Sustainable Development and Policy Journal*, forthcoming

[15] "Carbon Colonialism," *The Equity Watch Newsletter*, 25 October 2000, www.cseindia.org/html/cmp/climate/ew/art20001025_4.htm

[16] L Lohmann, "The Carbon Shop - Planting New Problems," WRM Plantations Campaign Briefing No. 3, 2000

[17] J Randerson, "Tree Planting Projects May Not Be So Green," *The Guardian*, 23 December, 2005

[18] P Granda, "Carbon Sink Plantations in the Ecuadorian Andes," *Accion Ecologica*, May 2005, www.sinkswatch.org/pubs/faceEcuador.pdf

[19] "Evaluation report of V&M Florestal Ltda. and Plantar S.A. Reflorestamentos, both certified by FSC - Forest Stewardship Council" World Rainforest Movement, November 2002, www.wrm.org.uy/countries/Brazil/fsc.html

[20] E Caruso and V B Reddy, "The Clean Development Mechanism: Issues for Adivisi Peoples in India," Forest People's Programme, April 2005 www.sinkswatch.org/pubs/cdm_&_adivasi_peoples_india_apr05_eng.pdf

[21] from the Carbon Neutral Company website, www.carbonneutral.com/pages/projectlocations.asp

[22] from the Carbon Clear website, www.carbon-clear.com/projects.htm

[23] from the Climate Care website, www.climatecare.org/projects/countries/index.cfm

Chapter 4: Three Case Studies in the Majority World

[1] See for instance, "Encountering Development: The Making and Unmaking of the Third World" by A Escobar.

[2] W. Bello, "Meltzer Repot on Bretton Woods Twins Builds Case for Abolition but Hesitates," *Focus on Trade* 48, April 2000

[3] S Bond, "Carbon Credits Critiqued," Edie News Centre, 1 September 2006, www.edie.net/news/news_story.asp?id=11953&channel=0

[4] J Ferguson, "The Anti-Politics Machine: "Development," Depoliticization, and Bureaucratic Power in Lesotho" 1994, University of Minnesota Press

[5] L Lohmann, "Carbon Trading: A Critical Conversation on Climate Change, Privatisation and Power," *Development Dialogue* no.48, September 2006

[6] D Hall and E Lobina, "Pipe Dreams," WDM and PSIRU, March 2006, www.wdm.org.uk/resources/briefings/aid/pipedreamsfullreport.pdf

[7] "The Rock Band Capitalist Tool For Cutting CO2," *Time Magazine*, 03 April 2006

[8] from the Carbon Neutral Company website, www.carbonneutral.com/coldplay/

[9] R Bayon, "From Ugandan Schoolteacher to International Carbon Consultant," The

Ecosystem Marketplace, 18 November 2005

[10] A Dhillon and T Harnden, "How Coldplay's green hopes died in the arid soil of India," 30 April 2006, *Sunday Telegraph*

[11] *ibid*

[12] *ibid*

[13] from private correspondence

[14] A Dhillon and T Harnden, "How Coldplay's green hopes died in the arid soil of India," 30 April 2006, *Sunday Telegraph*

[15] *ibid*

[16] S Dagar, "Money From Thin Air," 07 May 2006, www.india-today.com/bto-day/20060507/features1.html

[17] *ibid*

[18] from the Climate Care Website

[19] This section is an expanded and updated version of an article that first appeared in the *New Internationalist* magazine in July 2006. The full report, "A funny place to store carbon: UWA-FACE Foundation's tree planting project in Mount Elgon National Park, Uganda" By Chris Lang and Timothy Byakola, published by the World Rainforest Movement is available for download at www.wrm.org.uy/countries/Uganda/Place_Store_Carbon.pdf

[20] "Compensate now!" GreenSeat website: http://www.greenseat.com/us/boekmod-pag1.asp

[21] Interview with Alex Muhwezi in Mbale by Timothy Byakola, Jutta Kill and Chris Lang. 19 July 2006.

[22] Denis Slieker (FACE Foundation), comment by e-mail on a draft version of the article "Uprooted" for *New Internationalist*, 19 May 2006.

[23] Interview with Fred Kizza by Timothy Byakola, December 2004.

[24] Interviews carried out at Mount Elgon by Timothy Byakola, December 2004.

[25] Telephone interview with Denis Slieker, Director FACE Foundation, by Chris Lang. 15 May 2006. Although he did not say so, Slieker is paraphrasing SGS's Public Summary of its FSC Certification Report of the UWA-FACE project, which states: "A Social Impact Assessment was undertaken and written up in September 2000. It found that local people did not clearly distinguish between the impacts arising from the gazzettement [sic] of the National Park and activities of the project. On further investigation, no significant social impacts were caused by the project." SGS (2002) "Mount Elgon National Park Forest Certification Public Summary Report," SGS (Société Générale de Surveillance) Forestry Qualifor Programme, Certificate number SGS-FM/COC- 0980, page 25. www.sgs.com/sgs-fm-0980.pdf.

[26] Musoke, Cyprian (2004) "MPs set demands on Elgon Park land", *New Vision*, 30 June, 2004. http://www.newvision.co.ug/D/8/17/369170

[27] Wambedde, Nasur (2002d) "Evicted Wanale residents now live in caves,

mosques", *New Vision*, 15 April 2002. www.newvision.co.ug/D/8/26/8796

[28] Interview with Cosia Masolo by Timothy Byakola, December 2004.

[29] SGS (2002) page 9.

[30] Telephone interview with Niels Korthals Altes by Chris Lang, 12 May 2006.

[31] Niels Korthals Altes (GreenSeat) and Denis Slieker (FACE Foundation), "Comments on a draft version of the article "Uprooted" for *New Internationalist*", 17 May 2006.

[32] *ibid*

[33] *ibid*

[34] Telephone interview with Denis Slieker by Chris Lang, 15 May 2006.

[35] Action Aid (no date) "Benet community in Kapchorwa win landmark case against land rights abuse". www.actionaid.org/uganda/955.html and Action Aid (no date) "Benet win land rights battle". http://www.actionaid.org/index.asp?page_id=691

[36] Wamanga, Arthur (2004) "45 Mbale park 'encroachers' detained," *New Vision*, 4 February, 2004. http://www.newvision.co.ug/D/8/13/337697

[37] Telephone interview with Denis Slieker by Chris Lang, 15 May 2006.

[38] E-mail from Ruud Bosgraaf (Press Officer Amnesty International Dutch Section) to Chris Lang, 16 May 2006.

[39] Email response from Tom Morton, Director of Climate Care on 12 May 2006.

[40] Climate care annual report. 2004. Available at www.climatecare.org

[41] Interview with Charles Marthinus, Director of Innovate Energy Projects on 4 May 2006.

[42] Interviews with recipients of the light bulbs in Guguletu were conducted on 7 May 2006.

[43] *Ibid* Asmal

[44] Interview with Prof. Dieter Holm on 4 May 2006.

[45] *Ibid* Holms

[46] Interview with Guguletu resident on 7 May 2006.

[47] Climate care annual report. 2004. Available at www.climatecare.org

Chapter 5: Celebrities and Climate Change

[1] T Meyer, "Media Democracy: How the Media Colonise Politics," Polity, 2002

[2] See RJ Butler, BW Cowan and S Nilsson "From Obscurity to Bestseller: Examining the Impact of Oprah's Book Club Selections" *Publishing Research Quarterly* 2005, 20(3):23-34

[3] J Agrawal, and W Kamakura "The Economic Worth of Celebrity Endorsers: An Event Study Analysis" *Journal of Marketing* 1995, 59(3):56-62

[4] G McCracken, "Who Is the Celebrity Endorser? Cultural Foundations of the

Endorsement Process" *Journal of Consumer Research* 1989, 16(3):310-21

[5] D Jackson and T Darrow, "The Influence of Celebrity Endorsements on Young Adults' Political Opinions" *The Harvard International Journal of Press/Politics* 2005, 10:80-98

[6] P David Marshall, "Celebrity and Power: Fame in Contemporary Culture", Minnesota, 1997; on individualisation within contemporary society more generally, see Zygmunt Bauman "The Individualized Society" Polity, 2001

[7] P Bond, D Brutus, V Setshedi, "Average White Band," July 2005, *Red Pepper*, www.redpepper.org.uk/global/x-jul05-whiteband.htm

[8] S Hodkinson, "G8, Africa Nil," November 2005, *Red Pepper*, www.redpepper.org.uk/global/x-nov05-hodkinson.htm

[9] S Hodkinson, "Geldof 8 - Africa nil: how rock stars betrayed the poor," October 2005, *Z Magazine*, www.newint.org/features/geldof-8/9-11-05.htm

[10] I Shivji, "Making poverty history or understanding the history of poverty," July 2005, *Pambazuka News*, www.pambazuka.org/en/category/comment/29009

[11] S Hodkinson, "G8, Africa Nil," November 2005, *Red Pepper*, www.redpepper.org.uk/global/x-nov05-hodkinson.htm

[12] O Reyes, "They Owe It All To Their Fans," July 2005, *Red Pepper*, www.redpepper.org.uk/arts/x-jul2005-celebrity.htm   Roy's recent statements have been even more critical about the misuses of celebrity as a means to embody popular struggles: "I am not such an uninhibited fan of Gandhi. After all, Gandhi was a superstar. When he went on a hunger strike he was a superstar on a hunger strike. But I don't believe in superstar politics. If people in a slum are on a hunger strike, no one gives a shit." Cited in R Ramesh, "Live to tell" *The Guardian*, 17 February 2007

[13] from the Philip Pullman website, January 2006, www.philip-pullman.com/pages/content/index.asp?PageID=120

[14] see http://southcentralfarmers.org/

[15] from an Amazon Watch press release, 8 October 2003, www.texacorainforest.org/trialofcentury.htm

[16] see www.matthewherbert.net

[17] see www.robnewman.com

Chapter 6: Positive Responses to Climate Change

[1] H Osborne, "New standards will raise carbon offset costs," *The Guardian*, 18 Jan 2007

[2] *ibid*

[3] F Harvey, "Billions lost in Kyoto carbon trade loophole," *The Financial Times*, 8

February 2007

[4] P Bond and R Dada (eds), *Trouble in the Air Global - Warming and the Privatised Atmosphere*, Centre for Civil Society (South Africa) and Transnational Institute (The Netherlands) (2005)

[5] See www.gotoalexanders.co.uk/eco.html

[6] *ibid*

[7] *ibid*

[8] From private correspondence

[9] From private correspondence

[10] www.palangthai.org/en/about

[11] "Demand side management entails actions that influence the quantity or patterns of use of energy consumed by end users, such as actions targeting reduction of peak demand during periods when energy-supply systems are constrained. Peak demand management does not necessarily decrease total energy consumption but could be expected to reduce the need for investments in networks and/or power plants." From the wikipedia page http://en.wikipedia.org/wiki/Energy_demand_management

[12] "Combined heat and power (or cogeneration) is the use of a heat engine or a power station to simultaneously generate both electricity and useful heat. Cogeneration is thermodynamically the most efficient use of fuel. In separate production of electricity some energy must be rejected as waste heat, whereas in separate production of heat the potential for production of high quality energy (electricity or work) is lost." From the wikipedia page http://en.wikipedia.org/wiki/Cogeneration

[13] See www.palangthai.org/en/bget and www.palangthai.org/en/about

[14] "Gas Flaring in Nigeria: A Human Rights, Environmental and Economic Monstrosity," A report by the Climate Justice Programme and Environmental Rights Action/Friends of the Earth Nigeria, June 2005, www.climatelaw.org/gas.flaring/report/exec.summary.htm.

[15] L Brownhill and T Turner, "Climate Change and Nigerian Women's Gift to Humanity," 17 October 2006, www.ukzn.ac.za/ccs/default.asp?2,40,5,1153

[16] *ibid*

[17] *ibid*

[18] L Lohmann, *Carbon Trading: A Critical Conversation on Climate Change, Privatisation and Power*, Development Dialogue no.48, September 2006

Further Reading

Larry Lohmann, 'Carbon Trading: A Critical Conversation on Climate Change, Privatisation and Power,' Development Dialogue no.48, Dag Hammarskjöld Foundation (2006)
Download from www.thecornerhouse.org.uk/pdf/document/carbonDDlow.pdf

Chris Lang and Timothy Byakola, '"A funny place to store carbon": UWA-FACE Foundation's tree planting project in Mount Elgon National Park, Uganda.' The World Rainforest Movement (2007)
Download from www.wrm.org.uy/countries/Uganda/book.html

The July 2006 issue of the *New Internationalist* magazine on carbon offsets
Available at www.newint.org/issues/2006/07/01/

Patrick Bond and Rehana Dada (eds), 'Trouble in the Air Global - Warming and the Privatised Atmosphere,' Centre for Civil Society and Transnational Institute (2005)
Download from www.tni.org/books/troubleintheair.htm

Leigh Brownhill and Terisa E. Turner, 'Nigerian Commoners' Gifts to Humanity: Climate Justice and the Abuja Declaration for Energy Sovereignty," paper presented, under the title, "Ecofeminist Action to Stop Climate Change," at the International Society for Ecological Economics (ISEE) Ninth Biennial Conference, "Ecological Sustainability and Human Well-Being," in Delhi, India, December 15-18, 2006
www.carbontradewatch.org/news/0612_nigerian_commoners_gifts_to_humanity.html

Cheat Neutral - A spoof offsets website - www.cheatneutral.com
"When you cheat on your partner you add to the heartbreak, pain and jealousy in the atmosphere. Cheatneutral offsets your cheating by funding someone else to be faithful and NOT cheat. This neutralises the pain and unhappy emotion and leaves you with a clear conscience."

TNI and Carbon Trade Watch

Founded in 1974, TNI is an international network of activists and researchers committed to critically analysing current and future global problems. Its goal is to provide intellectual support to grassroots movements concerned about creating a more democratic, equitable and sustainable world.

Carbon Trade Watch is a part of the Environmental Justice project of TNI and promotes a critical analysis of the use of market-based mechanisms as a means of dealing with climate change, from both the perspective of their impact on local communities and their lack of effectiveness. By centring its work on bottom-up community-led projects and campaigns, Carbon Trade Watch provides a durable body of research which ensures that a holistic and justice-based analysis of climate change and climate policy is not forgotten or compromised. Carbon Trade Watch is an active participant in the Durban Network for Climate Justice.

The Environmental Justice project aims to unveil existing injustice issues of land use and conflict, pollution, water issues, deforestation and agriculture, through in-depth research, multi-media work, linking issues, education and the promotion of transnational solidarity.

www.carbontradewatch.org

www.tni.org

To receive information about TNI's publications and activities, we suggest that you subscribe to our bi-weekly bulletin by sending a request to: tni@tni.org or registering at www.tni.org

To receive a monthly bulletin about news, reports and information about the world of emissions trading, carbon offsets and environmental justice, send an email to kevin@carbontradewatch.org or register at www.tni.org/ctw